A DANGEROUS HOPE

ENCOUNTERING THE GOD OF GRACE

AL TRUESDALE AND BONNIE PERRY

Beacon Hill Press of Kansas City
Kansas City, Missouri

Copyright 1997
by Beacon Hill Press of Kansas City

ISBN 083-411-6804

Printed in the
United States of America

Cover Design: Paul Franitza
Cover Photo: Superstock

Library of Congress Cataloging-in-Publication Data
Truesdale, Albert, 1941-
    A dangerous hope : encountering the God of grace / Al Truesdale
and Bonnie Perry.
        p. cm.
    ISBN 0-8341-1680-4
    1. Grace (Theology)   2. Christian life—Nazarene authors.
I. Perry, Bonnie.   II. Title.
BT761.2.T78   1997
234—dc21   97-33509
                                                                      CIP

10   9   8   7   6   5   4   3   2   1

CONTENTS

How blessed is God! And what a blessing he is!
He's the Father of our Master, Jesus Christ,
and takes us to the high places of blessing in him.
Long before he laid down the earth's foundations,
he had us in mind, had settled on us as the focus of his love,
to be made whole and holy by his love.
Long, long ago he decided to adopt us into his family
through Jesus Christ.
(What pleasure he took in planning this!)
He wanted us to enter in the celebration
of his lavish gift-giving by the hand of his beloved Son.

(Eph. 1:3-6, TM)

FOREWORD

Grace. There is no sweeter word in any language. And there is no grander word in all the theological books of the world.

Only one other word is its equal: *love.* And both *grace* and *love* uniquely describe our wonderful Creator, God, and Savior, as Al Truesdale so beautifully explains in the following pages.

God's grace is the most wonderful revelation a person can experience. It comes at that crucial point in life each of us must reach when we realize that no matter how hard we may try and accomplish, we cannot save ourselves, that we really have nothing to offer God, and that we are total spiritual paupers. I sometimes describe myself as a depraved termite on a speck of a small planet, which is a speck in our solar system, which is a speck in our galaxy, which is also less than a speck in the vastness of the universe, only one of more than 100 billion other galaxies.

Without grace, that is all we are—actually nothing. Only the love and grace of God declare that we are more than that. That He would create us in the first place as objects of His grace is amazing. That He would redeem us from our sins by His own blood is even more amazing. Further, that He would choose to indwell us and make us joint heirs with the Second Person of the Godhead is mind-boggling.

As are many, are you sometimes gripped with your own inadequacy and unworthiness? This book will help you understand God's grace and lift you to new heights of joy in Him.

Or are you self-satisfied with your moral lifestyle and perhaps many works of righteousness? You will learn that these things, while good, add nothing to God's grace, for which you are as unworthy as all of us.

May God use this book to grant us all a fuller understanding of His amazing grace. And may this cause us to love, praise, and worship Him all the more for what Al Truesdale calls God's wonderful "extravagance" toward us.

—Dr. Bill Bright
Founder and President
Campus Crusade for Christ International

INTRODUCTION

In this tightly packed, well-executed, and appropriately illustrated volume, Albert Truesdale and Bonnie Perry combine their theological and literary talents to give cogent expression to John Wesley's vision of the God of grace and the redeeming hope that arises from that vision. God's gracious presence and care, Wesley believed, suffuses both the created order and human existence, and, since He is sovereign, the gracious God will finally redeem the world polluted by human sin when the children of God are revealed and glorified at the eschaton (Rom. 8:17-30).

With Wesley, the authors understand God's sovereignty to be the sovereignty of *love* (1 John 4:8). God is self-giving, self-sacrificing *agape* (vv. 9-10). Love is of His very *nature*. God's *power*, like all His other attributes, is an expression of His *love*. The Holy One is holy *love*. His sovereign love expresses itself in righteousness, in covenant-making and covenant-keeping, and finally in the New Covenant. Such, they argue, is the historic revelation of the God of grace. John Wesley was not rationally formulating a theological *proposition;* he was declaring a *biblical faith* derived from the story of God's dealings with His firstborn son Israel that climaxed in His definitive self-revelation in the person and work of His Son (Heb. 1:1-4). For Wesley, Jesus' whosoever will was untrammeled by any hidden dogma of absolute predestination. His gospel was Paul's optimism of grace of Rom. 5:12-21. It was not "free will theism"; it was a *biblical* doctrine of *free grace*—God's grace "free *to* all and free *in* all" that becomes justifying, sanctifying, and finally glorifying grace when we believe in Christ Jesus, who became what we are in order that we (by the Spirit we receive through Him) might become what He is (1 Cor. 1:30; Rom. 8:1-17).

Such is the Wesleyan vision of God's grace so effectively recounted in these pages. Truesdale and Perry are persuaded that the 18th-century English reformer still offers serious theologians a true "middle way" between Reformation and Catholic understandings of salvation and holiness—a gospel of *living hope* for both the

Church and the world. Wesleyan theology, they argue, functions within the dynamic tension between the *already* (the kingdom of grace) and the *not yet* (the kingdom of glory). Entire sanctification is understood in these pages as the finest flower of the present kingdom, understood not as sinlessness but as "love excluding sin," moral and spiritual *wholeness*. Christian holiness is always social, communal, confessional, sacramental, and open-ended. It is not of this world, but it *is for* the world. Yet such holiness is never here and now complete—it is but the prelude of God's final victory, when the kingdom of grace becomes the kingdom of glory. "For in this hope we were saved" (Rom. 8:24). Central to Wesleyanism is John Henry Newman's conviction: "Faith ventures and hazards; right faith ventures and hazards deliberately, seriously, soberly, piously, and humbly, counting the cost and delighting in the sacrifice." Right faith is indeed "a dangerous hope," like the hope of Jesus who gave himself to the death of the Cross in the joyous confidence that the Father would indeed raise Him from the dead.

—William M. Greathouse
Trevecca Nazarene University
Nashville

ACKNOWLEDGMENTS

We gratefully acknowledge our seven fellow pilgrims: Dan Braaten, Wes Eby, Susanna Fitzgerald, Mike Oyster, Sandra Parks, Rex Perry, and Esther Truesdale. Without your help, this project would not have come to be.

—Al Truesdale
Bonnie Perry

Faith ventures and hazards;
right faith ventures and hazards deliberately,
seriously, soberly, piously, and humbly,
counting the cost and delighting in the sacrifice.
—John Henry Newman

PROLOGUE

"The mystery which has been hidden from the past ages and genera-
tions; but has now been manifest . . . Christ in you, the hope of glory"
(Col. 1:26-27, NASB).

I first tasted *real* Carolina ham and beans around Al and Esther
Truesdale's dining room table. The secret is in the ham hocks, explained Al, as he strategically placed the Tobasco sauce in front of his
plate. During the months this book was being fashioned, I spent a
good deal of time around the Truesdale's dining room table. And
how to prepare good ham and beans wasn't the only thing I learned.

I learned that God is much bigger than I thought He was. That
if we believe what we say we believe about Him, our lives will
never be the same. I learned that the magnitude of His grace is as-
tounding. That if we dare to hope in Him—His essence and His
character, I mean—something deep inside us changes.

I learned that in God's kingdom I am not perched precariously
on the slippery ledge of the precipice of sin. That my spiritual walk
is not a disaster waiting to happen. And that living the holy life
can be more than wishful thinking.

I learned that God is sovereign. That the big picture is bigger
than I know. That ultimately evil will not overcome good. And that
the whole earth is filled with His glory.

I learned that God isn't afraid of tough questions. That His
love is filled with glorious promise. And that confession is a gift.

I learned that before the worlds were framed, God had already
chosen to make himself vulnerable. That following His example is
risky business because it costs a lot and it hurts sometimes. And
that living a life of faith in Him is a dangerous hope.

All this, and much more, I learned. This book was a team effort. It
was written through laughter and tears, in affirmation and confession,
on a journey of mutual discovery with six focus group members who
became fellow pilgrims on this incredible refashioning of our faiths.

We invite you to join us on this sojourn. Around God's table
(and the Truesdales') there's always room for one more. Grab a cup
of coffee and pull up a chair, won't you? Let's rediscover the God
of grace together. It's an encounter you won't soon forget.

—Bonnie Perry

Thus is God's grace free in all; that is, in no way depending on any power or merit in man, but on God alone, who freely gave us his own Son, and "with him freely giveth us all things."

—John Wesley
"Sermon on Free Grace"

O Almighty God, dear heavenly Father . . . grant us your divine grace that we might guard against all that does not serve the honor and glory of your holy Name.

—Martin Luther
"The Lord's Prayer"
Personal Prayer Book

Grace is ever and in all relations God's deed and act, taking place in this and that moment of time in which God wills to be gracious to us, and is gracious, and makes His grace manifest.

—Karl Barth
The Holy Spirit and the Christian Life

CHAPTER *1*

The God of All Grace

IRVING DROVE A NEW YORK CITY TAXI FOR MORE THAN 28 years. Most of those days were relatively uneventful. But one sunny Monday morning in 1966 would be different. As he routinely drove a passenger toward La Guardia Airport, they began a casual conversation that would impact his life forever.

"How do you like driving a cab?" the passenger asked.

"It's OK," Irving replied. "If I could get a job making $100 more a week, I'd take it—just like you would."

"I wouldn't change jobs if I had to take a cut of $100 a week," the passenger said, explaining that he was a doctor in the neurology department at New York Hospital.

Irving had always been curious about people and tried to learn what he could from them. He had developed quite a rapport with many riders across the years. Perhaps it was that the doctor obviously loved his work; perhaps it was the mood of a spring morning. Irving decided to ask the rider for help.

"Could I ask a favor?" Irving began. The man didn't answer. "I have a son, 15, a good kid . . . he wants a job. Is there any possibility that you could get him some kind of summer job—even if he didn't get paid?"

The doctor didn't reply for a long time. "Have him send me his school record," he said finally. Irving wrote the address on his brown lunch bag.

It was an ordinary moment in an uneventful day, but the repercussions would last for years to come. Irving's son Robbie got the job, working for $40 a week that summer. It began a love affair with medicine. Today the cabby's son is Dr. Robert Stern, obstetrics-gynecology chief resident at Columbia Presbyterian Medical Center in New York City.[1]

Most every day we meet new people. Usually the introductions amount to no more than a social courtesy. We speak politely, recognizing that we may never see this person again. But sometimes, as in Irving's case, introductions have a profound impact on us. We accept a blind date and meet the person who will become our spouse. We become acquainted with someone who later becomes part of the genius behind a successful business venture. We sit in class on the first day of school and are introduced to a teacher who will significantly impact our thinking or change our pattern of life.

In the Bible, God engages us in the most penetrating and transforming of all conversations.

Occasionally introductions form clear lines of demarcation in our lives. "That was before I met Sarah!" we might say, or "Because of that conversation, I have changed my entire business philosophy."

The Bible makes many introductions to persons and events. Some are minor; others lead to rich and continuing conversations. Obviously the most significant introduction in the Bible is that of God himself. God reveals himself in His Word, and when we make acquaintance with Him, there we begin a journey in which we come to know not only God but ourselves, our neighbor, and the world around us as well. For the revelation of God is also the revelation of humankind.

In the Bible, God engages us in the most penetrating and transforming of all conversations. Sometimes He speaks directly, usually through a spokesperson—Moses or Elijah, for instance. But much of the biblical conversation between God and His creation uses the language of divine deeds. Through the interchange between God's deeds and humanity's faithful interpretation of them, we begin to discover who He is and who we are to be. Ultimately in the person of Jesus the Christ, God's deeds and His Word become one. His character, personality, and actions on behalf of humanity are consistently and definitively revealed in Jesus' life and ministry.

As God reveals himself in the Bible, there is an attraction to

His candor. The Bible doesn't sugarcoat the fact that the people God chose as the primary community through which to reveal himself were often slow learners. The biblical writers let us look in on the Israelites' 40-year journey in a wilderness land, a sojourn brought on largely by their unbelief. In Scripture we meet not only the prophet Isaiah, who gave up everything to follow God, but also Jacob, who was sometimes more interested in wealth than obedience. The Bible doesn't hide the sin of David, Israel's greatest king. It candidly records a painful crisis of faith endured by seventh-century prophet Habakkuk. And perhaps most astonishing of all, the Bible doesn't for one moment conceal that the "chosen people" had a bad habit of turning away from the God who had chosen them. In Scripture, the family's secrets are exposed— the triumphs of faith and the lamentable defeats, the glory and the shame. In them we see ourselves. And amidst Israel's often-fractured journey with God, He makes himself known.

We too come to know God within the context of our own histories, parts of which are appealing and parts of which are appalling.

The biblical writers find it unnecessary to hide anything, and so should we. Like Israel, we too come to know God within the context of our own histories, parts of which are appealing and parts of which are appalling. No matter—we don't have to hide our stories to be included in God's story of redemption.

Through the narration of Scripture, we know that God gave himself to the slave-nation Israel. We know that in the revelation of himself, God has established a reputation for reaching out to the unlovely and moving them toward transformation. We know He has a habit of showing up in the strangest places with promises of deliverance, hope, and reconciliation. He is the God of *grace*.

The Gracious God

Grace is one of the pivotal terms the Bible uses to describe God's character. It reveals the way He relates to His creation and describes His love in action. Love isn't only something God "does"; love is what God *is* (1 John 4:8). We can't point to some tangible essence behind love and say, "That's God." Any true statement that can be made regarding God is in some sense a comment on His love. When we speak of God as righteous, faithful, long-suffering, and merciful, we are referring to dimensions of His love.

In His presence there is only one appropriate attitude—worship.

To say that God is love means that the fundamental power undergirding the creation, maintenance, and government of the world is love—self-giving and self-sacrificing love (1 John 4:9-10). God's sovereignty is a sovereignty of love; He is not arrogant, capricious, or vengeful. God's love is gracious. God's grace is loving.

Often we speak or sing of God's grace as if it were a *thing*, a substance created and dispensed by God. But the grace of God is God *in action*. When we speak of someone's honesty, we know that we are describing a quality of the person, not a substance the person has generated. Likewise, in acting graciously God reveals himself. In His gracious deeds He declares His name, His essence *as* God.

The Holy God

The Bible declares that there is only one God who is the sole source of all that exists. All other pretenders to deity are impostors. In sharp contrast to the polytheism* of the surrounding nations, Israel learned that God is one, the *Holy One*. The central Old Testament affirmation regarding the oneness of God is called the Shema: "Hear, O Israel: The LORD our God, the LORD is one" (Deut. 6:4). God's oneness is not principally a matter of numbers, but of His being and nature. In the one holy God, deity is complete. After Him there is only creation. In the creation's relationship to Him there is only one appropriate posture—radical dependence. In His presence there is only one appropriate attitude—worship.

So when the biblical writers say that the one God is *holy*, they

---

*The belief that there are many gods, not just one God as the Bible teaches.

simply mean that God is God. The word expresses God's absolute "otherness." It is a term that belongs exclusively to God alone, for He alone is God. The holiness of God also means that He is the sole source of His own being. His existence and His value do not depend on His relationship to anything else. Swedish theologian Gustaf Aulén writes, "That God is the Holy One means . . . that in relationship to the world he is exalted and sovereign. God's 'holiness' establishes therefore a definite line of demarcation between the divine and the merely human."[2] Consequently, no part of the creation can be called holy unless God has associated himself with it as a channel for His own self-expression and purposes.

Through the prophet Isaiah, Yahweh, the God of Israel, sent the following message to His captive people: "This is what the LORD says—Israel's King and Redeemer, the LORD Almighty: I am the first and I am the last; apart from me there is no God. Who then is like me? Let him proclaim it" (44:6-7). God jealously guards His holiness, not because He is insecure, but because all efforts to share God's holiness are ridiculous and self-destructive. When any part of the creation attempts to be anything but creation, it falls. Isaiah mocks the ruler or nation that says, "I will ascend to heaven; I will raise my throne above the stars of God. . . . I will make myself like the Most High" (14:13-14). The results of such aspirations are, of course, disastrous: "But you are brought down to the grave, to the depths of the pit. Those who see you stare at you, they ponder your fate: 'Is this the man who shook the earth and made kingdoms tremble, . . . who overthrew its cities and would not let his captives go home?'" (vv. 15-17). When any part of the creation attempts to act like God, chaos follows.

The righteous God is the redeemer God.

The Righteous God

When we discuss God's *righteousness,* we often think in terms of moral perfection. But God's righteousness has nothing to do with an external moral standard that He measures up to. Just as we have seen with grace and holiness, righteousness is a facet of the character of God. It is the holiness of God in active expression. Righteousness describes the inner nature of God and the demands He makes upon His people because of His nature. God appears in the Bible as the One who loves justice and compassion (Amos 5:6-24; Mic. 6:6-8). Those who love God will love what God loves. They will want to imitate Him. The result should be a people who love justice, compassion, honesty, and fair dealing between persons.

The word *righteousness* also describes God's absolute faithfulness to himself and His creation. It entails the active declaration of His name and His comprehensive opposition to idolatry and all other forms of evil. We can consider it the part of His character that guards the purity of His holiness and love against infringements and depreciations. Any enterprise or idea that in the slightest measure places God in league with evil automatically departs from the righteous God.

As an expression of His love, God's righteousness goes far beyond mere opposition to evil. It seeks to redeem the offender, much as the Old Testament prophet Hosea sought after his adulterous wife, Gomer. He shows special consideration for the poor, the downtrodden, the stranger, the widow, and the orphan. He is benevolent, creative, and gracious. The righteous God is the redeemer God. The history of Israel and the life, death, and resurrection of Jesus Christ prove this beyond any doubt.

We begin to understand God's righteousness by what He does and how He behaves. The Hebrew word for law is *torah*. The Old Testament Torah, or the Law of the Lord, includes the Ten Commandments. But the Law of the Lord is not first of all a series of commandments issued by God. Primarily it is God's *way*—God's way of being and doing. The main emphasis of the Bible is not on knowledge *about* God, but on the imitation of God. This imitation occurs by following the right way of living, which in Hebrew is called *halakhah* (ha-la-KAH). The root meaning of the word is "to walk," to walk in the *way* the Lord walks. Simply, it means to *love* what God loves, to *do* what God does. *Halakhah* leads to an ever-increasing approximation of God's actions.[3] God's commandment that we follow in His way reflects His desire for us to conform to His character. Any independent way or alternative way is sin and leads to death.

The Lord registers His complaint against Judah through the

prophet Micah for not walking according to God's way: "In my own *actions* I showed you what is good. You have no excuse" (Mic. 6:8, author's paraphrase). Again in the New Testament God's people are admonished: "Since *God so loved* us, we also ought to love one another" (1 John 4:11, emphasis added). The Law is not merely something God commands; it is His *way* of being.

The God we have been describing is the God of all grace. What He commands He first of all gives. He gives himself creatively, redemptively, and sacrificially to His creation. As we reflect on God's grace, we join the psalmist's refrain:

I will give thanks to Thee, O LORD, among the peoples;
And I will sing praises to Thee among the nations.
For Thy lovingkindness is great above the heavens;
And Thy truth reaches to the skies.
Be exalted, O God, above the heavens,
And Thy glory above all the earth (Ps. 108:3-5, NASB).

Israel believed that the holy God who is "far off" (transcendent) is also "near" (immanent), and that he had invited his people into a special covenant relationship. . . . Israel's relationship to Yahweh was not that of a slave but that of a "first-born son" who had been graciously redeemed. Gratitude for this deliverance was the primary motive for Israel's response of faith.

—Bernard Anderson
Understanding the Old Testament

Human freedom is the God-given freedom to obey. Faith *is the obedience of the* pilgrim *who has his vision and his trust set upon God's free act of reconciliation. . . . This obedience in love and faith is the human response to the divine offer of justification, sanctification, and calling in Christ Jesus.*

—Karl Barth
The Humanity of God

*Now may the God of peace,
who brought back from the dead our Lord Jesus,
the great shepherd of the sheep,
by the blood of the eternal covenant,
make you complete in everything good
so that you may do his will,
working among us that which is pleasing in his sight,
through Jesus Christ, to whom be the glory
forever and ever.
Amen.*

—Heb. 13:20-21, NRSV

CHAPTER *2*

Covenant Maker, Covenant Keeper

$\mathcal{T}$HE 50TH WEDDING ANNIVERSARY CELEBRATION planned by the children of James and Hattie Hinton was one of the very few times the couple were ever in the limelight. They had worked hard all their lives, sacrificed for their children, paid for a humble home, and loved each other dearly. But no magazine had ever sought their story.

Surrounded by their family and friends, James and Hattie were simultaneously pleased and embarrassed by all the attention. Before the celebratory cake was cut and gifts opened, the master of ceremonies—their oldest daughter who drove down from Nashville—asked a question. "Mama and Daddy, how did you do it? How were you able to love each other so faithfully through 50 years, even when times were tough?"

James and Hattie shuffled nervously, each waiting for the other one to speak. Finally, James spread his feet, rammed his thumbs into the sides of his new overalls, and exclaimed, "Shucks, it warn't nothin'. Through thick and thin, we just kept on givin' ourselves to each other. Warn't nothin' more than that!"

The God of grace is a God of relationship. Through thick and thin He just keeps on giving himself to others, even though doing so is a very risky venture. The Bible reveals God to be a covenant maker and a covenant keeper.

Covenant is perhaps the defining theme of the Old and New

Testaments. Although the Old Testament uses the word in various ways, most of the time *covenant* is used to describe the relationship God establishes with His creation. God established a number of covenants in the Old Testament—with Noah, Abraham, Israel, and David. In the New Testament God establishes the new covenant in His Son, Jesus Christ.

Running through all these covenants are two affirmations. First, the whole world depends upon relationship with God, the Sovereign Lord, who always takes the initiative. Second, God is wholly gracious. He wills more good for us and for His world than we do for ourselves. Covenant demonstrates that all life of all creation is a gift. We are totally dependent on, and called into relationship with, the God who for no reason other than extravagant love called us into being. With unfailing love He has steadfastly given himself to us. All of God's covenantal relationships are bound together in love. "The earth," the psalmist affirmed, "is full of his unfailing love" (Ps. 33:5). Our lives and all creation are rooted in incomprehensible love. "I will be your God, and you shall be my people" (Jer. 7:23, NRSV. See also Exod. 6:7; Lev. 26:12; Deut. 29:13; Jer. 11:4; 30:22; 31:33).

In the ancient Near East a king would make a covenant with the ruler of a subordinate nation that owed allegiance to the king. These covenants or treaties included numerous elements, one of which was the set of obligations to which the subordinate bound himself. Another was a set of blessings and curses—the consequences for either obedience or disobedience to the covenant. The ancient political treaties are similar to the covenant God made with Abraham and the children of Israel at Sinai. Clearly, God is the One who takes the initiative in covenant making. God chose Israel—Israel did not choose God (Deut. 10:15), and the only explanation is God's love and faithfulness (7:7-9). Israel enters an all-inclusive relationship with God even as God gives himself without reserve to Israel. God listens to Israel, and Israel in return listens to God. God and Israel can make mutual claims upon each other. But neither one

What Abram could not do, God did for him.

can force the other to comply; neither one is a puppet in the hands of the other. God is called Israel's Father, and Israel God's son (Exod. 4:22; Deut. 32:6). But Israel must not take God's care for granted. The covenant blessings depend on Israel meeting the conditions, the obligations of the covenant. God, and God alone, is Israel's King.

Genesis 15 relates the establishment of a covenant between God and Abram (later called Abraham). In the ancient Near East it was customary for covenant partners to seal a covenant by slaying several animals (v. 9), halving them, laying the halves on the ground, and then walking between them. As they walked, the covenant partners swore allegiance to the covenant by saying something like this: "May I too be slain and cut in half like these animals if I am unfaithful to the terms of this covenant." According to Genesis 15, God told Abram to provide six animals, which Abram then killed. He cut the animals down the middle (the two birds excepted), laying each half side by side (vv. 9-12). As the sun went down Abram saw a smoking firepot and a flaming torch pass between the halves of the carcasses (vv. 17-18). These two fiery symbols showed that God himself had passed through the divided carcasses! What was the meaning? Given the ancient context, the significance is unmistakable. By passing through the halves, God—the Sovereign Creator—had said to Abram, if I am unfaithful to the covenant I have made with you, then may what has been done to these animals be done to Me also. The extent to which God enters and commits to the covenant astonishes and humbles us. The act staggers our comprehension; God took the initiative to identify with Abram and Israel. What grace! What love! What vulnerability! What depth of commitment!

If God had been interested in guarding against vulnerability, He certainly would not have loved sinners.

Why would God establish covenant with Abram? If He is holy as we have described Him, He certainly does not *need* to establish covenant with another as though there were some deficiency in Him. He makes and keeps covenant simply because He loves us and desires to do so. When God made the covenant with Israel, the people had done nothing special to deserve His favor. Yet He freely committed himself (for better or worse) to a community whose very existence would declare the name of the Lord in all creation.

The beauty of the covenant relationship is that the partners make themselves vulnerable (Ezek. 6:2-15). This is characteristic of a genuine love relationship. Love freely given takes the risk of being rejected, misunderstood, misused, or not reciprocated. In making covenant with Israel, God demonstrated His power and revealed His character through the vulnerability of His love. This is hardly what we would expect of a god. And yet if God had been interested in guarding against vulnerability, He certainly would not have loved sinners. God's choice to make himself vulnerable is simply another evidence of His holy love.

As is the case in all worthwhile love relationships, the covenant must be entered into and maintained freely. God's covenant partner, Israel, would not merely be a puppet in His hands. He would not force Israel to obey, even when Israel's rebellion caused Him great pain. Many times after having promised to live by the terms of the covenant, Israel would turn away from God to serve other so-called deities. Yet in spite of its disloyalty, God chose Israel. Why?

As the biblical record makes clear, God's choice of a covenant partner was not based on any particular merit found in the nation of Israel. Human wisdom might have expected that the Holy God would seek to covenant with a strong partner, a nation that had gained international prominence because of its wealth and power. Instead, God chose a people who, properly speaking, were not a people. Slaves in Egypt when He found them, the Israelites were downtrodden and fragmented, lacking all but the most rudimentary distinctions as a people.

God's covenant with Israel brings us face-to-face with His graciousness, His righteousness, and His creativity. Israel brought nothing of distinction to the covenant (Exod. 13:3, 14-16). At no point could Israel say to God, "You chose us because we deserved to be chosen, because of our righteousness, or because You recognized that on our own we had already accomplished much of what You were seeking." Yet God intended to make Israel an active participant, a real dialogue partner, in the covenant. Everything God would accomplish in and through His people would spring from His own resources, His own holy love, and His grace. In the process, Israel was supposed to learn how to worship the Holy One, how to repeat His deeds by living righteously before others and in harmony with God's creation.

Unfortunately, God's people had a difficult time keeping the story straight.

God's plan for the nation Israel would set it in sharp contrast to its neighbors. Hierarchies of power and privilege characterized the surrounding nations. In those social orders the strong members of society could and did exploit weaker members. Social pyramids placed the "losers" at the bottom and stacked the elite at the top because of the wealth and power they brought to the social arena.

But what if the foundations of the social order were radically different? Could a nation survive when everyone, regardless of historical "accident" (physical weakness, gender, intelligence, wealth) or divine assignment (priest, prophet, king, court official) followed a different model? What if the judges, farmers, artisans, business persons, and the king were to think of themselves and their place in society by first recalling their radical poverty before God? What if in assessing their worth they were to begin by recognizing that all of it was a gift from God? And what if the social structures—and a person's role in them—were seen primarily as means through which the *way* of the Lord could be made known and His name declared?

No less than this is what God intended for Israel, His special people. Through them, God would reveal himself as the Holy and Gracious One. He would excite the nations to worship Him and would teach all people how to live according to the *way* of the gracious God. By fulfilling the terms of the covenant, Israel would make graciousness the foundation of its social and individual existence.

Unfortunately, God's people had a difficult time keeping the story straight. Like Jonah at Nineveh, they had a bad habit of thinking that God had chosen Israel because He loved no others or because of its own righteousness. They forgot that the grace of God expresses His holiness and is not an excuse for permissive, sinful behavior. The Old Testament keeps a sad but faithful record of the ways in which the people abandoned the terms of the covenant, forgot to look at other members of the community graciously, adopted the social structures of other nations, and ruinously exploited the weaker members of society. As the prophets Amos and Micah make clear, Israel often ignored the relationship between worshiping God and acting with mercy and justice toward one's neighbor. And according to Jeremiah and Amos, Israel began to think that so long as the sacrifices were properly made, caring for widows and orphans or conducting honest business transactions were not important.

The New Covenant God

The God of the Old Testament shows up again in the New Testament. From beginning to end, the New Testament writers carefully declare that the God who became incarnate in Jesus of Nazareth is none other than the Holy One of Israel, who dealt graciously with Abraham. Jesus' own mother magnifies God by recounting the mighty deeds of mercy He had performed for His people. Mary declares God's goodness when she visits her cousin Elizabeth, whose unborn child (John the Baptizer) leaps for joy at the sound of Mary's voice. We call her song the Magnificat. From generation to generation, Mary declares in her song, God has scattered the proud, brought down rulers, lifted the humble, filled the hungry with good things, and sent the rich away empty. "He has helped his servant Israel," she exults, "remembering to be merciful to Abraham and his descendants forever, even as he said to our fathers" (Luke 1:54-55). In the presence of such a merciful God, Mary responds appropriately. She worships: "Holy is his name" (v. 49).

He who is the Messenger is the Message.

In the Old Testament, God speaks through His mighty deeds and faithful messengers. But there is always a distinction between the message and the messenger. In the New Testament the distinction disappears. He who is the Messenger is the Message. Not only does Christ proclaim the good news of God—He *is* the good news of God. According to the Gospel as recorded by John, "In the beginning was the Word, and the Word was with God, and the Word was God. He was with God in the beginning. Through him all things were made; without him nothing was made that has been made" (1:1-3). Then John tells us, "The Word became flesh and made his dwelling among us" (v. 14). John's theme is echoed in Colossians where we are told that Christ "is the image of the invisible God, the firstborn over all creation. For by him all things were created: things in heaven and on earth, visible and invisible, whether thrones or powers or rulers or authorities; all things were created by him and for him. He is before all things, and in him all things hold together" (1:15-17).

Jesus' obedience is an act of worship.

The Incarnation is the mystery of God becoming flesh. In the Church, we recognize the incarnation of God in Jesus of Nazareth by a confession of faith. We affirm that Christ is fully human and fully God, that He is of one substance with the Father, and that He is one Person in whom the human and divine natures are not confused. But what we confess in faith we readily admit we do not fully comprehend. "No man has seen God at any time," John says. But "the only begotten God, who is in the bosom of the Father, He has explained Him" (1:18, NASB). We confess that through the Son and by the testimony of the Holy Spirit, God has definitively revealed himself.

Jesus himself affirms God's purposes for the Incarnation. At the close of His life on earth, He prays the high-priestly prayer recorded in John 17. "I have brought you glory on earth. . . . I have revealed you," He says (vv. 4, 6). According to Jesus, the primary reason the Son came into the world was to glorify His Heavenly Father through a faithful revelation of Him. As the obedient Son (Phil. 2:5-11), Christ perfectly declared and honored the holiness of

God. At no point in Jesus' ministry does He attempt to bring glory to himself or establish His own independent way. His mission is to reveal and glorify His Father.

As God's obedient Son, Christ did perfectly well what Adam and his children did poorly. Even under the most severe temptation, Christ refused to seize for himself what belongs to God alone. In the wilderness Satan urged Jesus to try to force the Father to prove himself: "Throw yourself down from here [the highest point of the temple], for it is written, 'He will command his angels concerning you, to protect you'" (Luke 4:9-10, NRSV). But Jesus would not yield. He would not from a position of finitude dictate how God should be God. "Do not put the Lord your God to the test," Jesus said (v. 12). "Worship the Lord your God and serve him only" (v. 8). Even when Jesus faced death on the Cross, He continued to obey God. Anticipating the horrors of the trial and Crucifixion, Jesus prayed, "Father, if

"In a way, we were dead and we knew it."

you are willing, take this cup from me; yet not my will, but yours be done" (22:42). His obedience fulfilled His mission.

Jesus' radical dependence on the Father models the relationship that was supposed to exist between God and His creation. From beginning to end, Jesus' obedience is an act of worship. By contrast, beginning with Adam, all people have turned away from the worship of God. We have gone our own way. By our disobedience we have boasted of our own self-sufficiency and declared our independence from God. The apostle Paul said that no one is excluded from God's judgment—neither Jew nor Gentile. All persons have followed in Adam's sin, and this is God's first judgment against us. Let "every mouth . . . be silenced, and the whole world . . . be held accountable to God" (Rom. 3:19, NRSV).

Our failure and Christ's faithfulness are supremely confirmed in the Resurrection. "He was not abandoned to the grave, nor did his body see decay," Peter said on the Day of Pentecost. For "God has raised this Jesus to life, and we are all witnesses of the fact" (Acts 2:31-32). "Therefore God exalted him to the highest place and gave him the name that is above every name," Paul writes later (Phil. 2:9).

The glorious salvation offered to all persons through the Holy Spirit results from the Son's faithful obedience and His desire to glorify the Father. The gospel of redemption—and our participation in it—is for the glory of God. Through the redemption that Christ has won (Col. 2:13-15), we are restored to the relationship with God that He intended for us all along. As we worship Him and turn from our self-centeredness, we begin to occupy our rightful place as His covenant partners. If the chief reason for which the Son came into the world was to declare the Father's glory, then the chief goal of our salvation is the same.

The pages of the New Testament sing out the good news that in Christ God acted graciously toward us. The gospel is stated clearly in John 3:16-17: "For God so loved the world that he gave his one and only Son, that whoever believes in him shall not perish but have eternal life. For God did not send his Son into the world to condemn the world, but to save the world through him." As one who had been transformed by the gospel, the apostle Paul repeated the substance of John's words: "Because of his great love for us, God, who is rich in mercy, made us alive with Christ even when we were dead in transgressions—it is by grace you have been saved" (Eph. 2:4-5). Through Christ we have unencumbered access to God.

Elie Wiesel, witness to the Nazi holocaust, writes about his experiences in *The Kingdom of Memory*. His story is a beautiful parable of God's grace and human response. As a teenager, Wiesel was imprisoned in Auschwitz, Birkenau, Buna, and finally Buchenwald. He describes the horrifying conditions of the death camp at Buchenwald. "In a way, we were dead and we knew it," he writes. Forty-five years later, Wiesel asked the American soldiers who freed him: "Do you remember, friends? In Lubin and Dachau . . . Ravensbruck . . . and Auschwitz, you were surrounded by sick and wounded and hungry wretches, barely alive, pathetic in their futile attempts to touch you, to smile at you, to reassure you, to console you and most of all to carry you in triumph on their frail shoulders; you were our heroes, our idols: tell me, friends, have you ever felt such love, such admiration?"[1]

God is a covenant-making, covenant-keeping God.

Confidence in God's grace and knowledge of it makes Christians glad and bold and happy in dealing with God, and with all his creatures; and this is the work of the Holy Ghost in faith.

—Martin Luther
Luther's Works, 6:451-52

The deity of the living God is revealed in its meaning and its power in the context of His history and dialogue with humankind, and thus in His togetherness with us. It is a matter of God's sovereign togetherness with humankind.

—Karl Barth
The Humanity of God

Now through your mercy implant in our hearts a comforting trust in your fatherly love, and let us experience the sweet and pleasant savor of a childlike certainty that we may joyfully call you Father, knowing and loving you, and call on you in every trouble. Watch over us that we may remain your children and never become guilty of making you, dearest Father, our fearful judge, changing ourselves, your children, into your foes.

—Martin Luther
"The Lord's Prayer"
Personal Prayer Book

CHAPTER *3*

Between the Being and the Doing

MANY PEOPLE WHO HEARD JESUS RECEIVED HIM GLAD-ly. His proclamation that God lifts up those who are lowly and contrite in spirit was welcome news to them. But not everyone was ready for Jesus. Perhaps the greatest irony of the New Testament is that those who were waiting most anxiously for the coming of God's Messiah did not receive Him (Matt. 25:41-46). Instead, those who believed they were hopelessly excluded from God's favor because they could not measure up to the standards imposed by the religious elite were the very ones to whom the gospel came. A gospel of grace was bad news to one group and good news to the other.

Good News, Bad News

Jesus used three parables in Luke 15 to illustrate this truth. From the beginning of His public ministry, tax collectors and sinners had clamored to be near Jesus and hear His gracious words. But the "righteous" Pharisees and teachers of the Law were repelled by the way He received sinners and seemed to delight in their fellowship. Jesus could not possibly be God's Messiah—He was extending the kingdom of God to "nobodies."

Understanding the Pharisees' dilemma, Jesus told them the parables of the lost sheep, the lost coin, and the lost son. The lost son of Jesus' story was a "nobody" too. Having squandered an early inheritance on wild living, he ended up wishing he could share food with a herd of pigs. Finally in desperation he decided to go home and ask to be employed as a hired hand. But while he was still beyond the gate, his father—full of grace—ran to meet him. "Bring the best robe. . . . Bring the fattened calf and kill it," the father declared joyfully. "For this son of mine was dead and is alive again; he was lost and is found" (Luke 15:22-24). The celebration caused much dismay for the older, "more righteous," brother. He wasn't planning to share his inheritance with a sinful "nobody" like this.

In Luke 18 Jesus told another parable "to some who were confident of their own righteousness" (v. 9). Two men went to the Temple to pray. One was a hated tax collector for the Romans, a publicly certified sinner and religious reject. The other was a Pharisee. Convinced that God would be happy to greet him, the Pharisee proceeded to the front of the Temple and began to announce his religious credentials to God. The tax collector, on the other hand, would not even lift his head before the Lord. "God, have mercy on me, a sinner," he prayed (v. 13). Jesus' summary of the parable captures the gospel message: "I tell you that this man [the tax collector], rather than the other, went home justified before God. For everyone who exalts himself [before God] will be humbled, and he who humbles himself will be exalted" (v. 14).

Had Jesus rebuked the Pharisees? Or had He complimented them?

On yet another occasion Jesus tried to communicate the gospel to the unheeding religious leaders. In Matt. 9 the Pharisees rebuked Jesus for eating with tax collectors and sinners. Jesus' reply might have left the Pharisees shaking their heads in confusion: "It is not the healthy who need a doctor, but the sick. But go and learn what this means: 'I desire mercy, not sacrifice.' For I have not come to call the righteous, but sinners" (vv. 12-13). Had Jesus rebuked the Pharisees? Or had He complimented them? Were they really the healthy ones who needed no doctor? Or were they the sickest of all, so convinced of their health they didn't recognize their need for God's grace? The Pharisees' declaration of their own spiritual health was really a rejection of the gracious God and His gospel of grace. You see, Jesus operated on the truth that the root of sin is embedded in the human spirit. That the root of sin is a refusal to worship God and acknowledge our radical dependence on Him. Jesus knew that we humans try to elevate ourselves—our resources, religiosity, moral accomplishments, and social standing—into a position that God alone can occupy. The Pharisees' refusal to recognize their own sickness confirmed Jesus' judgment against them.

The Christ who ate and fellowshipped with tax collectors and sinners was God Incarnate. He is the same God who made a covenant with Hebrew slaves, urged Hosea to reclaim his prostitute wife, and traveled to Babylon to redeem a captive people who had landed there because of their backsliding. Had the religious leaders reconsidered the history of Israel's gracious journey with God, they might have understood. But the Pharisees had prepared for one God—and another one, the God of grace, showed up.

Jesus' proclamation of the God of all grace opened the door to reconciliation with the Father. He offered eternal life to those who would surrender their claims of self-righteousness and self-reliance. He opened the door for all people, but many would not walk through it.

Not every Pharisee missed the gospel message, though some received it after Jesus' death and resurrection. None of the New Testament writers seemed to have grasped the meaning of God's grace more clearly than did the apostle Paul. But before Paul became an apostle of grace, he vigorously pursued the ways of the Pharisees. We first meet him in the Book of Acts holding the clothes of those who were stoning Stephen for his faith in Jesus. By Paul's own admission, he was responsible for the deaths of many early believers. But all of that changed on the road to Damascus when Paul had a saving encounter with Christ.

Before sin expresses itself in wrong ways of doing, it is a wrong way of being before God.

According to Paul, all persons—both Gentiles and Jews—

stand under God's judgment (Rom. 3:9-20). To a Pharisee, such language was scandalous. The scribes and Pharisees prided themselves on the clear distinction between the sinful Gentiles who practiced idolatry and the righteous Jews who possessed and obeyed the Law of Moses. Clearly the Gentiles deserved God's judgment and wrath, for they did not know and worship the Holy One of Israel. But to their horror they heard Paul pronounce the same judgment on Jews.

The Being and the Doing

Paul's insight into why God's judgment rests on both Gentiles and Jews is a keystone of the New Testament. Through the centuries it has helped the Church understand why the gospel is directed to all persons, and why faith in Christ is the only way to be reconciled to God. The Book of Romans is Paul's most complete statement of the gospel. Church reformers such as Augustine, Martin Luther, John Calvin, and John Wesley have appealed to Romans to recapture the gospel message.

Paul understood that it is misleading to concentrate on the more obvious and odious sins of the Gentiles. Before sin expresses itself in wrong ways of *doing,* it is a wrong way of *being* before God. Through his own journey, Paul learned that being in right relationship with God, being able to love God and one's neighbor, is principally a gift, not an accomplishment. Moreover, it is a gift that pronounces judgment on all our supposed accomplishments—especially the religious ones.

Echoing the words of Jesus, Paul taught that the Law was good because it had been given by God (Matt. 5:17-19; Luke 16:16-17; Rom. 7:7-12). He knew that the fundamental principle of the Law is that we ought to worship God with our whole soul, mind, and strength, and that we should love our neighbors as we love ourselves (Matt. 22:36-40; Luke 10:25-28). The New Testament never disparages the Law itself. Instead, the writers condemn a wrong use of the Law or a wrong relationship to it. Paul painfully discovered that even though the Law is good, and even though what it calls for—worship and love—is essential, *the Law cannot deliver that for which it calls.* "Therefore no one will be declared righteous in his sight by observing the law" (Rom. 3:20), Paul declares. Rather, through trying and failing to fulfill the Law, we become conscious of sin.

Paul tried diligently to *do* what the Law calls for, attempting to earn his way into God's favor. A "Pharisee of the Pharisees" he called himself in Acts 26—"exhibit A" in the case for self-righteousness. But Paul failed miserably. As a Pharisee in pursuit of righteousness, he could obey the outward form of the Law. He could successfully refrain from taking God's name in vain or from dishonoring the Sabbath. But he could not truly worship God and love his neighbor as the Law demanded. His every effort to accomplish this goal landed him in deeper despair. With each attempt he became more aware of his sinfulness. And although Paul wasn't committing gross acts of the flesh, consciousness of sin held him fast in its grip. "What a wretched man I am!" he cried. "Who will rescue me from this body of death?" (Rom. 7:24).

> *Religious pride is sin that pretends to be what it is not— a friend of God.*

What was Paul's problem? What is our problem? Paul was trapped by sin's essence. *Despite his good intentions, all his attempts to "do" his way into God's favor only revealed his sinful self-righteousness instead of a faithful dependence on God.* Again the essence of sin is *a declaration of independence from God*—whether we say it with our mouths or demonstrate it in our lives. Immorality is not sin's principal signature—that designation goes to unbelief, self-righteousness, and self-sufficiency.

Paul learned through much anguish that he was powerless to perform his way into God's favor. He couldn't love as he ought, and his supposed religious accomplishments were just so much "rubbish" (Phil. 3:7-11). Paul was a sinner, and his very religiosity had confirmed it.

Religious pride is sin that pretends to be what it is not—a friend of God. The sin of the Gentiles, on the other hand, could easily be smoked out. Their idolatry, sexual license, murder, and so on, were overt declarations of independence from God. Not so with religious pride. It travels in the most impressive garb and in the most impressive company. Nevertheless, Jesus was a master at detecting and naming it: "Woe to you, teachers of the law and Pharisees, you hypocrites! You are like whitewashed tombs, which look beautiful on the outside but on the inside are full of dead men's bones and everything unclean. In the same way, on the outside you appear to people as righteous but on the inside you are full of hypocrisy and wickedness" (Matt. 23:27-28).

When Paul understood the truth of his inability to perform for God, he became a ready candidate for the gospel of grace. For his tortured question, "Who will rescue me from this body of death?" (Rom. 7:24), Paul received a glorious answer: "Thanks be to God—through Jesus Christ our Lord!" (v. 25).

Paul understood our propensity to pharisaism.

Clearly, what God commands He must give. This is true because of the faithfulness of His nature. To receive the gift of reconciliation through Christ, we must become repulsed by our sinfulness, renounce our own paltry efforts to earn favor with God, and admit that we are powerless to break the bondage of sin and guilt. We must be prepared for a radical reordering of our self-understanding and our loyalties according to the values of the kingdom of God. All this is included in the New Testament view of repentance.

So for Paul "there is no difference [between Gentile and Jew], for all have sinned and fall short of the glory of God, and are justified freely by his grace through the redemption that came by Christ Jesus" (Rom. 3:22-24). Human efforts contribute nothing to reconciliation with God. Righteousness is His gift to us. "Where, then, is boasting? It is excluded. . . . [on the principle] of faith" (v. 27).

Does this reconciliation with God that comes by grace and faith in Jesus Christ now set aside the Law? Not at all, says Paul. The gracious God makes possible in us what the Law upholds but cannot deliver: love for God and neighbor. Listen to Paul's excellent summary: "Therefore, since we have been justified through faith, we have peace with God through our Lord Jesus Christ, through whom we have gained access by faith [which is itself a gift from God] into this grace in which we now stand" (Rom. 5:1-2).

As a recipient of God's righteousness instead of being a prisoner of his own failures, Paul's disposition before God had been radically altered: "You see, at just the right time, when we were still powerless, Christ died for the ungodly. . . . God demonstrates his own love for us in this: While we were still sinners, Christ died for us" (Rom. 5:6, 8). For Paul, humility, reconciliation, and hope have now replaced arrogance, guilt, and despair. Righteousness by faith will yield the fruit of holiness and eternal life (6:22).

Sometimes the same malady that afflicted Israel and the Pharisees plagues Christians: we forget that we, too, were slaves in Egypt. We begin to review our accomplishments and compliment God for having chosen such worthy covenant partners. When we do, sinners are disdained, adulterers are stoned, and Pharisees stride confidently to the front of the Temple.

Paul understood our propensity to pharisaism. He announced the good news of righteousness by grace and faith to two groups of persons: those who had not been reconciled to God by grace, and those who had. The Galatian believers were in danger of straying away from Christ without realizing it. Because of misleading instructions they were receiving, they were beginning to add some of the old Jewish practices to the gospel of grace. Paul reminded them that radical dependence upon a gracious God—living in the righteousness that comes by grace alone—is not only the way we *enter* the kingdom of God but also forever the only basis for our *continuing* there. He carefully warned the Galatians against attempting to complete by human effort what the Holy Spirit had begun (Gal. 3:3).

More important than the warning is the promise that through the Holy Spirit's empowerment, we can both begin and continue to journey with the God of grace. We can authentically abide in the Spirit. The gracious God is now our hope, our life, and our peace.

O love divine, what hast Thou done?
Th' immortal God hath died for me!
The Father's coeternal Son
Bore all my sins upon the tree;

Th' immortal God for me hath died!
My Lord, my Love is crucified.
—Charles Wesley
"O Love Divine,
What Hast Thou Done?"

———

God's deity is revealed in His freedom for love, and
thus His capacity to be not only in the heights but also in
the depths, not only great but also small, not only in and
for Himself but also with another distinct from Himself,
and to offer Himself to humankind.
—Karl Barth
The Humanity of God

———

No person living is without some prevenient grace,
and every degree of grace is a degree of life. . . . No one sins
because he has not grace, but because he does not use the
grace which he has.
—John Wesley
The Letters of John Wesley,
VI, IV (3rd Jackson ed.)

CHAPTER 4

A Holy Encounter

MOST OF US HAVE HAD THE DELIGHT OF WATCHING A loving, attentive mother care for her infant. She treats her child ever so gingerly, being careful to support the head and not to twist an arm or a leg. She makes sure that the child is fed on time and is cautious that no rashes or signs of illness go unnoticed. One fascinating dimension of such parental care is that the child is not even aware of all the attention he or she is receiving. Nevertheless, the mother regularly initiates punctual and periodic care. That the infant is unaware of all the goings-on has no effect on the mother's diligence. She has more than the moment in mind. Her diligence is moved by a design. She hopes that as the child grows and his or her consciousness emerges, the nurture will produce a healthy, loving, and socially integrated person.

A mother's care for an infant can serve as a parable for helping us understand how the God of grace reaches out and gives himself to humanity. Jewish theologian Abraham Heschel wrote eloquently of "God in search of man." The patience with which God "searches for humanity" staggers our comprehension. The Old Testament prophets never tired of celebrating God's mercy and long-suffering care for Israel. And the Bible leaves no room for doubt regarding who initiates the search. As Jesus illustrated in the parables of the lost sheep and the lost coin (Luke 15:3-10), humanity is not the first searcher—God is. He is the active God of love. There is no record in either the Old or the New Testament of any person ever initiating a search for God. But the record of the gracious God searching for, finding, and giving himself to humanity marches unbroken from Genesis to Revelation.

Many times in the biblical record the person God seeks doesn't even know he or she is lost. God sought Adam and Eve for their companionship in the cool of the evening. He found Abraham in Haran and promised to lead him to a Land of Promise. He sought Jacob at the fork of the river Jabbok, when Jacob was preparing to meet his brother Esau, whom he had defrauded. He found Jonah at the bottom of the sea—and then Nineveh, much to Jonah's displeasure. God found the nation of Israel when it was a captive in Babylon and brought it home as He had promised. Ultimately, God takes the initiative and becomes incarnate in Jesus of Nazareth. In Christ He *finds* all the captive members of Adam's race and makes atonement for the sin of the world (Col. 2:13-14). "Because of his great love for us, God, who is rich in mercy, made us alive with Christ even when we were dead in transgressions—it is by grace [we] have been saved" (Eph. 2:4-5).

> *There is no record in either the Old or the New Testament of any person ever initiating a search for God.*

A Spontaneous Love

Long before any of us are aware of God's gracious activity in our lives, He is present and active. His initiative on our behalf does not depend on our being conscious of it. It is not based on our merit; that is, we can't earn it. God reaches out to us and gives himself to us just because He wants to (Titus 3:5-6). His love is *spontaneous*. It breaks forth by itself. And it breaks forth universally, without respect for the arbitrary divisions among persons that sinful humanity has imposed. God will not be hemmed in by religious, racial, national, or cognitive barriers.

Jesus' disciples had a difficult time thinking of God in this way. So He gave them a lesson in the nature of God's love, commanding them to love their enemies and to pray for those who persecuted them. By this they would show themselves to be children of God, because they would reflect God's character. Jesus said that the Heavenly Father "causes his sun to rise on the evil and the good, and sends rain on the righteous and the unrighteous" (Matt.

5:45). God extends His love and care indiscriminantly—even though His doing so sometimes angers those who believe that He should love us based on our performance.

Jesus soundly answered these objections in the parable of the farmer and his vineyard. Early in the morning a certain farmer hired a group of workers and agreed to pay them one denarius, a day's wage. Then, three more times during the day the farmer hired additional workers, some even late in the afternoon. When evening came, the owner of the vineyard instructed his pay clerk to pay the workers, beginning with the last hired. Amazingly, the farmer paid the same amount to each worker—those who had labored hard all day and those who had worked only as little as one hour. Not surprisingly, those who had worked all day thought this arrangement very unfair.

Fair indeed! God's grace is scandalous . . .

"Don't I have the right to do what I want with my own money?" the farmer answered the protesters. "Or are you envious because I am generous?" (Matt. 20:15).

An even more widely known parable of God's grace is the Luke 15 account of the prodigal son. The elder brother strongly objected when his father extended forgiveness to the younger son, who had disgraced the family name. "It's not fair," he contended.

Fair indeed! God's grace is scandalous to anyone who insists He pay attention to the petty efforts we make to earn His favor. Interestingly, sometimes we Christians find ourselves identifying with the workers who began early in the morning or with the elder son who stayed home. When we do, Jesus might respond by asking, "How did you draw that mistaken conclusion? I had identified you with the workers who came in the eleventh hour. You're more like the prodigal son than the elder brother!" Of course, He would be correct.

Set Free to Face the Truth

Although it is true that the good news regarding God's grace should be announced to those who have not yet returned home, it must also be declared over and over to those of us who have received the gospel. Once we are in the Kingdom by God's grace, the basis of our remaining there does not change. As magnificent as the transformations are that the Spirit of God effects in us, they never become the basis of our acceptance before God. Just as grace is the *entryway* to the Christian life, it is also the *pathway* of the Christian life. No matter what God accomplishes through us, grace will always be the way God encounters us. Katherine Hankey expressed this truth when she wrote,

Tell me the old, old story
Of unseen things above —
Of Jesus and His glory,
Of Jesus and His love.

Tell me the story simply,
As to a little child.

We now understand that our position before God rests solely on the riches of His grace and not on our own righteousness. Our acceptance is not based on our performance. As a result, we can be set free to face the truth about ourselves on a continuing basis and to confess our failures to God, to ourselves, and, where appropriate, to others. Martin Luther said that life in the kingdom of grace is characterized by "a continuous and unceasing forgiveness of sins, both that which we receive from God and that which we exercise mutually in forebearing and edifying one another."[1] As we shall see, life lived in the strength of God's grace is characterized by both an ongoing transformation into Christlikeness and an increasing awareness of the need to confess our sins. If our vision of the Christian life is missing either of these elements, our faith is crippled. To put the matter another way, a correct understanding of God's grace makes *transformation* and *confession* not only necessary, but possible. Thanks be to God!

A Self-Giving Love

Another facet of God's spontaneous love is that it is *self-giving*. When extending to us His grace and mercy, God in fact gives himself. As we saw in the first chapter, love is not principally something that God *does*—love is what God *is*. As God loves, He expresses himself. And as God expresses His love, He opens the way for those He loves to have fellowship with Him.

As we have seen, any love that is self-giving is love that takes risks. Love makes itself vulnerable. Almost instinctively we know that love cannot exist apart from vulnerability—the risk that it might be rejected, might not be appreciated for what it is, and might not be reciprocated.

In the Old Testament we find many expressions of God's vulnerable, self-giving love. No instance is more captivating than the account of Hosea's love for his prostitute wife. Through Hosea's love for Gomer, who disappointed him repeatedly, God hoped to instruct Israel regarding the character of His love. And though God desired to win Israel's faithful love, clearly there was no guarantee that His love for Israel would be returned in kind. Of course, the ultimate expression of God's vulnerable love is through His incarnation in the life, death, and resurrection of His only Son. "In this the love of God was made manifest among us, that God sent his only Son into the world, so that we might live through him. In this is love, not that we loved God but that he loved us and sent his Son to be the expiation for our sins" (1 John 4:9-10, RSV). Charles Wesley gave powerful expression to the vulnerability of God's love made incarnate in Christ:

Although we can experience the grace of God, we cannot comprehend it.

> He left His Father's throne above,
> So free, so infinite His grace!
> Emptied Himself of all but love,
> And bled for Adam's helpless race.
> 'Tis mercy all, immense and free,
> For, O my God, it found out me!

In some small measure we try to understand the grace of God by thinking of our own love for a spouse, a child, or a friend. But our comparisons quickly stumble in the presence of God's love. Although we can experience the grace of God, we cannot comprehend it. It is unfathomable. Language fails to take its measure. Yet the apostle Paul prayed that the Ephesian Christians would be rooted and established in love, that they would be able to grasp how wide and long and high and deep the love of Christ is. Then, paradoxically and correctly, he prayed that they would "know this love that surpasses knowledge" (3:19). The more our understanding of God's love grows, the more unfathomable it becomes.

When we regard the magnificence of the creation, we catch a glimpse of how God gives himself to us before we are even aware of it. The Book of Genesis tells us that God created the heavens and the earth. The Epistle to the Hebrews affirms that the world was formed by God's command alone (11:3). And the letter to the Colossians tells us that even now the world holds together because of Christ's creative presence (1:17). In Him the world receives both its origin (John 1:1-3) and its future (Rom. 8:19-22). So just as God created the world, He sustains and directs the world. All are the work of His grace.

In *Pilgrim at Tinker Creek* American novelist Annie Dillard tells how she learned to view the world graciously. She readily admits that much in nature doesn't fit into a neat scheme (floods that destroy livelihoods or diseases that afflict innocent children). And though she recognizes the grace of God in na-

Long before we ever move toward Him, God has already moved toward us.

ture, she says, because of the fierceness of natural evils, she sometimes rides "a bucking faith." Nevertheless, Dillard says she has seen "the light" of divine glory and grace in the trees, in the changing colors of Tinker Mountain, and in the rolling clouds of a winter's evening. She invites her readers to "knock, seek, ask." "Read the fine print," she says, and God's creation will "catch you up . . . and you'll come back . . . transformed in a way you may not have bargained for. . . . The universe was not made in jest but in solemn incomprehensible earnest. By a power that is unfathomably secret, and holy, and fleet. There is nothing to be done about it, but to ignore it, or see."[2]

The psalmist would have understood and agreed with Dillard intuitively: "The heavens declare the glory of God; the skies proclaim the work of his hands. Day after day they pour forth speech; night after night they display knowledge" (19:1-2). The apostle

Paul would have echoed Dillard's appeal: "For since the creation of the world God's invisible qualities—his eternal power and divine nature—have been clearly seen, being understood from what has been made" (Rom. 1:20).

The Grace That Goes Before

Long before we were able to identify God's presence or focus on His deeds, He was active. No one is a stranger to God. Long before we ever move toward Him, God has already moved toward us. Even when we do respond, He makes the response possible. We speak of this dimension of God's activity as prevenient grace or the grace that goes before.

The sacrament of infant baptism is one way the Body of Christ recognizes and affirms the prevenient workings of God—before the child even knows that she or he is the object of God's love. Infant baptism is also a decisive moment in which the church and the child's parents, guided by the Holy Spirit, recognize their responsibility for nurturing the grace of God in the developing child. The church accepts responsibility for being the kind of community in which the gospel can be heard and responded to. The church accepts responsibility for reminding the child that God's love and mercy have already made a claim on him or her and that God's efforts to redeem him or her will continue.

There are no chance or aimless encounters with God.

The Gospel of John says of Christ that He is "the true light, which enlights everyone" (John 1:9, NRSV). God's prevenient grace is universal; it reaches to all persons everywhere. Some Christians believe that the purpose of prevenient grace is only to preserve the world and society against chaos. They don't believe that all people are candidates for divine redemption, and so they attach only limited significance to God's activity in those who, they believe, are not destined for salvation. However, many other Christians, including those informed by the theology of John Wesley, believe the Bible clearly teaches that God's redemptive love is extended to everyone. Wherever people are, God wants them to come to repentance and to inherit eternal life. The Holy Spirit works preveniently, patiently, and intentionally in all persons to prepare the way for their hearing the gospel.

Probably some of the most remarkable stories you've ever heard recount the ways God works preveniently to bring persons to a saving encounter with himself. As far as surprises are concerned, no aspect of God's creativity surpasses this arena of His activity. There are no chance or aimless encounters with God. Former slave trader John Newton called it "amazing grace." As Christians we can offer ourselves as channels through which the Holy Spirit will work to lead persons to repentance. We can help provide an environment at home, school, or work that will heighten a person's sensitivity to the Holy Spirit. But we must never make the mistake of trying to set the terms by which the free Spirit of God will act. He will surprise us every time, and He will explode any channels we try to dig for Him. "The wind blows wherever it pleases. You hear its sound, but you cannot tell where it comes from or where it is going. So it is with everyone born of the Spirit" (John 3:8). The Holy Spirit is the free Spirit of God, who searches and knows the hearts of all persons.

The good news of creative grace is that God does not retreat from chaos.

In some persons the prevenient work of God may have been so successfully cultivated and received that they have never really known themselves to be anything other than children of grace. Receiving Christ as their Savior may be largely a matter of intentionally confirming for themselves the Christ whose presence has attended them even before they were ever aware of it. For them, becoming Christian may be far less dramatic and decisive than it is for others. Some of these people may not clearly remember a time when they were not a Christian, when they did not love God.

As Christians, our message to all persons everywhere should be that the God of creative grace can penetrate the most tragic of

personal histories and can give forgiveness and hope where before there was only guilt and despair. The good news of creative
grace is that God does not retreat from chaos. Sovereign love
means that though finite efforts may quickly reach their limits,
God the Creator does not quit. True, He will not redeem by coercion. He is not a bully or tyrant. Coercion is weaker than love any-
way. "Love," Paul said, "bears all things, believes all things, hopes
all things, endures all things. Love never ends" (1 Cor. 13:7-8, RSV).
Without qualification, the cross of Christ proves that this is true of
God.

All the blessings which God hath bestowed upon man are of his mere grace, bounty, or favour; his free, undeserved favour; favour altogether undeserved; man having no claim to the least of his mercies. It was free grace that "formed man of the dust of the ground, and breathed into him a living soul," and stamped on that soul the image of God.

—John Wesley
Sermon: "Salvation by Faith"

The divine act of forgiveness appears to faith as an inscrutable miracle. It does not occur in accordance with human thinking and expectations, but contrary to what we may expect or think.

—Gustaf Aulen
The Faith of the Christian Church

[For John Wesley] justification by grace through faith remains the only foundation for the divine-human relationship throughout the whole course of sanctification. . . . Justification provides the substructure for refashioning life in this world through sanctification.

—Theodore Runyon
Sanctification and Liberation

CHAPTER 5

Great Expectations

SHARON AULT TELLS OF HER FIRST VISIT TO THE GRAND
Canyon. With very limited resources, she remembers, her parents
had saved and planned for months to take the family of five all the
way from Mississippi to Arizona. Sharon tells how she spent months
anticipating the journey. Her expectations were heightened by pic-
tures and stories. She says that her child-sized capacity for anticipation fairly exploded as she waited. Then came the journey. For days
they traveled. Finally they arrived in Arizona and drove to the
canyon rim. The rush of emotion that overwhelmed her as she gazed
out over the splendor and majesty of the Grand Canyon is an experience she will never forget.

"My expectations were so inadequate!" she recalls thinking.
"The Grand Canyon is so much more than I thought it would be!"
Later, reflecting as an adult on the event, she said: "My anticipations had expanded as much as they could. The reality simply
overwhelmed my expectations."

The New Testament writers were keenly aware of the rich history of God's faithfulness to Israel. From childhood they had
learned the story of God's journey with His people. Along with
their fellow Jews, they had inherited the promises of God made
through the prophets. Now, they believed, the same God who once
initiated and maintained the old covenant had fulfilled His
promises by establishing a new covenant through Jesus Christ.

As faithful witnesses to the gospel of Christ, the New Testament writers spoke as persons overwhelmed by an event that had
eclipsed their greatest expectations. The good news of the gospel

was more than they or any of their fellow Jews—including the prophets—could have imagined. In Christ, they proclaimed, God has acted surprisingly and decisively to redeem His creation (Rom. 15:8; Heb. 12:18-24). In Jesus of Nazareth the kingdom of God has come!

Though the New Testament writers told the story faithfully, they were communicating a reality that was still too large for them to comprehend (Rom. 11:33). They could not have anticipated the riches of grace poured out by the Father through His Son in the power of the Holy Spirit. The old wineskins simply could not contain the gospel (Matt. 9:17). Yet, though the gospel Jesus preached marked a sharp advance over the Old Testament, the new story is continuous with the old. The story of Jesus is the story of the one God who is holy love.

He is the kingdom of God.

The phrase "the kingdom of God" does not appear in the Old Testament, but the concept runs through much of it. Yahweh is the King of Israel (Exod. 15:18; Num. 23:21; Isa. 43:15). He is the Lord over all the earth (2 Kings 19:15; Isa. 6:5; Jer. 46:18; Pss. 29:10; 47:2; 93; 96:10; 97; 99:1-4; 145:11-21). He visits His people to manifest His rule among them and to demonstrate His rule over all creation (Ps. 96:10-13).

Again and again in the Old Testament, God is said to be the God "who comes" (a *theophany* [Ps. 98:8-9]). He came to creation (Judg. 5:4-5), to Abraham (Gen. 12:1-8), to Jacob (Gen. 32:22-30), to Sinai (Deut. 33:2, 5), and to the captives in Babylon (Isa. 40:1-11). And in coming, God revealed His purposes, His righteous judgments, His steadfast love, and His salvation. The theophanies reminded Israel of its covenant responsibilities. They showed Israel what it could expect God to do in the future.

While God is already King, the Old Testament looks forward to a time when God's Kingship over *all* the earth will be manifested and confirmed. All the nations will know the true God and will join Israel in worshiping Him. The Lord's salvation, given to the Jews, will be extended to the Gentiles as well: "'Shout and be glad, O Daughter of Zion. For I am coming, and I will live among you,' declares the LORD. 'Many nations will be joined with the LORD in that day and will become my people. I will live among you and you will know that the LORD Almighty has sent me to you'" (Zech. 2:10-11). When God's kingdom comes, all people will share in His covenant and follow the way of the Lord.

Not surprisingly, the prophets had diverse ideas regarding the shape of the coming Kingdom. Like Sharon Ault's expectations regarding the Grand Canyon, the prophetic descriptions of the coming Kingdom proved inadequate. The New Testament says the prophets had peered diligently into what they could not fully anticipate (1 Pet. 1:10-12).

Kingdom Come

What is this new story about the kingdom of God the New Testament writers tell? Mark, the writer of the first Gospel, begins an answer: "Now after John was arrested, Jesus came into Galilee, preaching the gospel of God, and saying, 'The time is fulfilled, and the kingdom of God is at hand; repent, and believe in the gospel" (Mark 1:14-15, RSV). In the person and preaching of Jesus, and through the Holy Spirit, the long anticipated kingdom or rule of God was inaugurated (Mark 1:15; Luke 17:20-22). Even now it is among us (Luke 17:20-22). Jesus is the Messiah, the Promised One in whom the Kingdom was to come. He proclaims the message of the kingdom of God. He *is* the kingdom of God. And what the Father has inaugurated in the Son, He will complete through the Son and by the Holy Spirit.

This is the new reality the New Testament writers proclaim. In Jesus Christ, the kingdom of God has come, and it is a Kingdom of universal grace! The kingdom of God is absolutely central to the Christian faith. Apart from the Kingdom there is no Good News. The Kingdom is the city set on a hill; it cannot be hidden. Jesus spoke of the Kingdom as a territory where one can enter or as a land in which one has a share. It is the treasure that comes down from heaven.

Many Christians try to separate the individual dimension of salvation from the Kingdom's much broader agenda. This is an error. The kingdom of God certainly includes individuals, but individual salvation by no means completes the Kingdom's vision. In fact, rather than speaking of the Kingdom being in us, we should first speak of our being in the Kingdom. Our citizenship in the kingdom of God is our reason for hope. And while the redemption of individuals is an important part of the kingdom of God, the New Testament is principally interested in telling how the Father has established this universal kingdom through His Son.

Not surprisingly, this gospel of the Kingdom that Jesus preached ignited controversy among His hearers (Luke 6:1-10; John 5:16-30; 6:60-71; 7:45-52; etc.). It was good news for some and bad news for others (Luke 4:14-30). The New Testament leaves no doubt that a kingdom of darkness exists that tries to obstruct the coming of the kingdom of God. And if some people missed Jesus' identity, the kingdom of darkness certainly did not (Mark 9:14-29; Luke 4:31-37; 8:26-36). The demons, who were opposed to God's Kingship, recognized Jesus as the Son of God. Satan unleashed every weapon —including death—against the Son of God. But Christ decisively defeated the kingdom of darkness. He didn't negotiate with it or explain it out of existence (Eph. 6:10-18; Rev. 12:10-12). Instead, God "disarmed the principalities and powers and made a public example of them, triumphing over them in [Christ]" (Col. 2:15, RSV).

The decisive defeat of Satan and all the powers allied with him is a part of God's redemptive activity. With the coming of Jesus, God's final act of salvation has been inaugurated, and it will be completed only when He has "reconcil[ed] to himself all things, whether on earth or in heaven, making peace by the blood of his cross" (Col. 1:20, RSV). "For he must reign until he has put all his enemies under his feet. The last enemy to be destroyed is death" (1 Cor. 15:25-26, NRSV). The New Testament admits there are many dimensions of the Kingdom that we don't yet understand and that await a future unveiling. And yet, those who enter the Kingdom live in its power *now*. They live in the sure hope that the Kingdom will be completed. This is the controlling and defining center of their existence.

A Kingdom of Nobodies

By earthly standards of power and prominence, the Kingdom Jesus inaugurated is a strange one indeed. It is a "kingdom composed of nobodies," John Crossan says. Just listen to the sort of people Jesus said would populate it.

1. The children and those who are willing to become like children (Matt. 18:1-4). In the first century, children were nobodies. Without social rank or power, they were absolutely dependent on their parents in every way. They had no rights of their own. It was an insult to compare an adult to a child.

"There goes the neighborhood!" someone might have answered Jesus.

2. The poor (Luke 6:20). It is difficult to imagine a more offensive description of kingdom inhabitants. "There goes the neighborhood!" someone might have answered Jesus. The poor about whom Jesus spoke were on the bottom of the social ladder, even below the peasant or artisan classes. They were the destitute ones, the beggars. By social standards of the time, the poor were considered unclean, degraded, and expendable.

3. The undesirables (Matt. 13:31-32). The parable of the mustard seed—such a very small seed—makes this description clear. People who aren't wanted anywhere else. The mustard shrub tends to grow and take over where it is not wanted. One ancient writer said that once the seed is sown it germinates quickly. Then it is difficult to rid a place of it. It gets out of control. And that, said Jesus, is what the Kingdom is like. It has "dangerous" takeover properties.

Now, add to all this the mourners, the meek, the hungry and thirsty, the merciful, the pure in heart, peacemakers, and the persecuted. "Does the list not improve at some point?" we might ask. "Doesn't it reach out to some really nice people?" No. And we still need to add those who, before Jesus touched them, were demoniacs, adulterers, prostitutes, and persecutors of Christ and the Church. And we mustn't forget the beggars infested with sores, tax collectors, prodigals, Samaritans, and shepherds. Is there any surprise that a sizeable number of people thought Jesus was demon possessed (Luke 11:14-20) and abandoned Him (John 6:60-66)? In the opinion of many, the people with whom Jesus often associated disqualified Him as one "sent from God."

When it came to defining and entering the Kingdom, the conflict between Jesus and the religious elite was fierce. To those who thought themselves unworthy to enter the Kingdom, Jesus called out, "Come on in!" To those who thought they had reserved the choice seats, Jesus said, "Forget it! The tax collectors and the prostitutes will enter the kingdom of God ahead of you" (Matt. 21:31-32).

Come and Die

So how does one get into the Kingdom? The New Testament calls everyone to enter and to do so at all costs (Matt. 13:44-45). But first, one must repent of his or her sins and submit to a radical transformation by the Kingdom's values. Before Dietrich Bonhoeffer died at the hands of the Nazi gestapo, he wrote, "When Jesus calls a man, he bids him come and die." His words were spoken in a national and religious context where the call to discipleship ordinarily meant no such thing. Bonhoeffer was simply being faithful to the words of his Lord. He knew that the terms for entering the Kingdom are uniform and they do not change.

. . . even now Christ is overthrowing the kingdom of darkness.

Jesus makes no "side deals" with anyone, regardless of his or her station in life, as His encounter with the rich young ruler demonstrates (Matt. 19:16-24). No one enters the Kingdom for whom the Kingdom is just a marginal interest. Nor does God leave it up to an individual or group to decide what life in the Kingdom will mean. That has already been determined by the God whose Kingdom it is. Entering the kingdom of God requires a radical reorientation of human life. The old selfish and sinful orientation must pass away, and a new orientation must replace it (Rom. 6:1-14). The old reality of sin must be judged and crucified; a new and creative reality must take its place.

In Flannery O'Connor's famous short story "A Good Man Is Hard to Find," we encounter the "Misfit" who has thought long and hard about what it would mean to follow Jesus. The Misfit concluded correctly that "If Jesus did what He said, then it's nothing for you to do but throw away everything and follow Him, and if He didn't, then it's nothing for you to do but enjoy the few minutes you got left the best way you can."[1] The Misfit was echoing Paul's words in 1 Cor. 15:12-19.

At one point in Jesus' ministry, John the Baptist wondered if Jesus and His kingdom were the real thing. Perhaps Jesus hadn't done what John had expected of Him. Perhaps the Kingdom didn't look like John thought it would. So John sent two of His disciples to Jesus and instructed them to ask some hard questions and then come back with some straight answers. Instead of sending a formal response to John, Jesus told the two messengers to stick around for a while. Afterward, He said, "Go back and report to John what you have seen and heard: The blind receive sight, the lame walk, those who have leprosy are cured, the deaf hear, the dead are raised, and the good news is preached to the poor." Then Jesus added, "And blessed is anyone who takes no offense at me" (Luke 7:18-23, NRSV).

Jesus meets two kinds of people in the Gospels: those who are poor in spirit and those who are not. Only the poor in spirit can enter the Kingdom. Recognizing their abject poverty before God, they release everything except His grace. They see the futility of living the old way—depending on their own strengths and abilities. Now, they wholeheartedly repent of their sins and cling to Him alone who can grant forgiveness. Set against Christ's authority, the kingdom of evil that opposed God's holy love is stripped of its preposterous claims. To enter the Kingdom, one must recognize that even now Christ is overthrowing the kingdom of darkness.

Candidates for the Kingdom are those who have despaired of all counter kingdoms—the ones they have created and the ones in which they have participated. They return to the Father of all mercy in the spirit of the prodigal son (Luke 15:11-24). Their efforts at kingdom-making have been shown for what they are—sinful and futile. They confess that the path of other kingdoms, other ways, leads to despair and death. The poor in spirit receive the gospel joyously and rush to enter the kingdom of God (Matt. 13:44-45). They are not disappointed. For just as Sharon Ault's vision of the Grand Canyon was too small, the God of all grace gloriously surpasses our greatest expectations.

*Jesus' proclamation of the "reign of God" does not in-
volve a demand for [persons] to follow a new, improved
moral code. It demands rather a radical decision for God.
The choice is clear either God and His reign or the world
and its reign. Nothing must prevent [us] from making this
radical decision between God and the world.*

—Hans Kung
The Church

---

*The plain scriptural notion of justification is pardon,
the forgiveness of sins. It is the act of God the Father,
whereby, for the sake of the propitiation made by the blood
of his Son, he "showeth forth his righteousness (or mercy)
by the remission of the sins that are past." . . . And from the
time we are "accepted through the Beloved," "reconciled to
God through his blood," He loves, and blesses, and watches
over us for good, even as if we had never sinned.*

—John Wesley
Sermon: "Justification by Faith"

---

*If you are a poor, distressed sinner, whose heart is
ready to sink for fear that God never will have mercy on
you, you need not be afraid to go to Christ, for fear that he
is either unwilling or unable to help you: here is a strong
foundation, and an inexhaustible treasure, to answer the
necessities of your poor soul; and here is infinite grace and
gentleness to invite and embolden a poor, unworthy, fearful
soul to come to it. If Christ accepts you, you need not fear.*

—Jonathan Edwards
"The Excellency of Christ"

CHAPTER 6

Living in Kingdom

The New Creation by Grace

NOW THERE WAS A MAN OF THE PHARISEES NAMED NICO-
demus, a member of the Jewish ruling council. He came to Jesus at night
and said, "Rabbi, we know you are a teacher who has come from God. For
no one could perform the miraculous signs you are doing if God were not
with him."

In reply Jesus declared, "I tell you the truth, no one can see the king-
dom of God unless he is born again."

"How can a man be born when he is old?" Nicodemus asked. "Sure-
ly he cannot enter a second time into his mother's womb to be born!"

Jesus answered, "I tell you the truth, no one can enter the kingdom
of God unless he is born of water and the Spirit. Flesh gives birth to flesh,
but the Spirit gives birth to spirit. You should not be surprised at my say-
ing, 'You must be born again.' The wind blows wherever it pleases. You
hear its sound, but you cannot tell where it comes from or where it is go-
ing. So it is with everyone born of the Spirit" (John 3:1-8).

Repeatedly the New Testament announces that those who enter the kingdom of grace become new persons, new creations. In
the Gospels and the Epistles, new creation is the gift of the Father,
made possible through Jesus and accomplished by the Holy Spirit.
Salvation is by grace through faith alone. As we have seen, this is
good news to the poor in spirit.

By Grace Alone

Even though Nicodemus was an authority on the Jewish Law

and a very prominent man in the religious hierarchy, he was not "poor in spirit." He did not possess that radical awareness of his poverty before God that could make him dependent upon grace alone. He was highly successful in the arena of human accomplishment, but he was blind to the kingdom of God. Clearly, Nicodemus should have understood that "that which is born of the flesh is flesh; and that which is born of the Spirit is spirit" (John 3:6, KJV). Entrance to the Kingdom requires going beyond Nicodemus's frame of mind.

Jesus could just as easily have been talking to Saul of Tarsus before his conversion. Like Nicodemus, Paul described himself as one who did not understand the new birth. He did not see that being re-created by Christ through the Spirit was his only hope for reconciliation with God (Rom. 7:13-24*a*; Gal. 1:13-17). So he plodded on in his futile efforts to establish his own righteousness—until he encountered Christ. He then understood that by his own fleshly efforts he could not gain freedom from the law of sin and death. The free gift of salvation comes only from God. Like so many others, Paul learned that God's kingdom is one of grace, not human accomplishment.

What was impossible before becomes a reality now.

Throughout the New Testament it is clear that God's gift of grace in Christ reconciles us to Him and sets us free from the law of sin and death (Rom. 8:1-2). It is equally clear that the same Spirit who reconciles (forgives, justifies) also accomplishes a profound transformation in us. The old passes away, and the new comes. God, who created the heavens and the earth, is present in Christ to re-create the penitent sinner (2 Cor. 4:6). The same God who raised Jesus from the grave will give new life—eternal life—to those who receive His Son.

The New Testament language is bold and sweeping: "Therefore, if anyone is in Christ, he is a new creation; the old has gone, the new has come! All this is from God, who reconciled us to himself through Christ" (2 Cor. 5:17-18). This is another way of saying that through the Spirit we are born anew. The creative Spirit of God actually changes the one whom He reconciles. What was impossible before becomes a reality now. Born anew, the regenerate person can worship God (Rom. 8:3-4) and can submit himself to continuing transformation by the Spirit (6:15-23).

Through Christ there comes both a changed *relationship* with God and a changed *person*. "To all who received him, to those who believed in his name, he gave the right to become children of God—children born not of natural descent, nor of human decision or a husband's will, but born of God" (John 1:12-13).

Through Faith Alone

We enter the Kingdom by grace. We enter the Kingdom by faith. By faith we mean *radical trust* in the person, Word, and promises of God. And just as grace is God's gift, so is faith (Phil. 3:7-11). The gift of faith comes through the action of the Holy Spirit upon us. He offers to open the Kingdom to us and makes it possible for us actively to receive the word of the gospel. Faith expresses itself in repentance and radical trust in the person and promise of God. It involves turning away from all that is opposed to the Kingdom and turning toward all the Kingdom is and will become. Karl Barth said that the faith by which we enter the Kingdom is "a glad and assured committal of ourselves to the goodness of God, who by His Word convicts us of our unbelief, at the cross of Christ."[1]

Often people have the notion that saving faith is something we muster up, a product of the human will.

Coming into God's kingdom by faith means we rely on nothing or no one but God for our salvation. Paul repeatedly uses the phrase "in Christ" (Rom. 6:11; 8:1; ["members of one body," Eph. 4:25]) to describe our radical dependence upon the person and work of Jesus. Often people have the notion that saving faith is something we muster up, a product of the human will. Not so. If it were, our reconciliation with God would be by works—our works. We might mistakenly believe we had something to boast about. To enter the kingdom of grace we must lay this, too, aside. Faith is a gift from God, as Paul makes clear in his letter to the Ephesian

Christians: "For by grace you have been saved through faith; and this is not your own doing, it is the gift of God—not because of works, lest any many should boast. For we are his workmanship, created in Christ Jesus" (2:8-10, RSV).

Now, as long as we remember that both grace and faith are God's gifts to us, we can talk about an active and obedient human response to the gift of faith. God empowers us to respond to the gift of salvation. We understand that no one can "will" himself or herself into God's favor. Apart from the work of God's grace, our wills as well as every other part of us are slaves to sin. But the Holy Spirit, who brings life, can empower us to embrace with purpose and resolution the reconciling grace of God. We exercise faith as a gift from God and through empowerment by the Holy Spirit. This is a paradox that is all too easily lost, either by those who turn faith into a human work, or by those who eliminate human participation from the redemptive process. The God of all grace need not eliminate or bypass a person's will in order to redeem him or her.

The gospel has nothing to do with nonsense.

The apostle Paul captured the paradox beautifully in his first letter to the Corinthians: "By the grace of God I am what I am, and his grace to me was not without effect. No, I worked harder than all of them—*yet not I, but the grace of God that was with me*" (15:10, emphasis added). Karl Barth put it this way: "Although faith can only be understood as the work of the Holy Spirit . . . it is still our own faith."[2] On another occasion Barth explained, "To hold to God thus always means that we receive everything wholly from God and so are wholly active for Him."[3]

There are numerous misconceptions regarding faith. Contrary to a popular misconception, faith does not amount to abandoning a higher order of certainty in favor of a weaker one. And faith does not mean treating the rationally or logically absurd as though they made good sense. The gospel has nothing to do with nonsense. Nor is faith mental assent to a body of religious doctrines. Instead, faith as radical trust means exchanging a lower order of reality for a higher one, and a lower confidence for a higher one—the person and word of God.

The writer of 1 John says that the Holy Spirit, who creates faith in us, also confirms to us that we have for Christ's sake become the children of God (Rom. 8:12-17; 1 John 4:13-15). The Spirit bears witness to our spirit that we are the children of God. When one lives in Christ by faith, Martin Luther said, "then it cannot be but that thine heart should laugh for joy, become free, certain, and courageous [and] sure that we have a gracious God."[4]

As treasured as the Spirit's witness may be, Christians must carefully guard against making the Spirit's witness the object of attention or the reason for confidence. Our confidence of faith doesn't rest in the Spirit's witness. Faith, the gift of God, is directed toward the One who raised Jesus from the grave. "My hope is built on nothing less . . ."

Life in the Spirit

Those who become new creations in Christ Jesus live in a new order and by a new power—the order of grace and the power of the Holy Spirit. As astonishing as it may sound, the Holy Spirit actually takes up residence in Christians (Rom. 8:9-11). He establishes the kingdom of God in us and bears witness to Christ through us. When we live by the power of the Spirit, we demonstrate the great difference between life according to the flesh and life according to the Spirit (Phil. 3:16-21; Col. 3:12-17; 1 Pet. 2:1).

The result of the Holy Spirit's transforming activity is what the New Testament refers to as "the fruit of the Spirit." Scripture identifies many of these, including "love, joy, peace, patience, kindness, goodness, faithfulness, gentleness and self-control" (Gal. 5:22-23). Not surprisingly, there is no exhaustive list. The New Testament writers could not have anticipated all the ways the free Spirit of God would reproduce the life of God in the Kingdom's citizens. We do know that the Spirit will reproduce in Jesus' disciples the fruit that announces the Kingdom's presence (John 15:1-5).

We have seen how Christ caught up the prophets' anticipations, transformed them, and fulfilled them more gloriously than even the prophets expected. What was true for the prophets is true for us. By the grace of God we can enter the Kingdom with joy and

confidence. By the grace of God our understanding of the Kingdom can expand indefinitely. But the meaning and power of the
Kingdom will always transcend human understanding, even as
God transcends our knowledge of Him. No one season or institution can ever take the Kingdom's measure. Just as the orbiting
Hubbel telescope has helped astronomers discover things about
the cosmos they didn't know before, so Christ must always be free
to call us into regions of the Kingdom we have not yet explored.

Grace That Works

Living in the Spirit actively places us in service to God. And
while it is true that works contribute nothing to our salvation, a
person who lives by the Spirit will practice a faith that works
through love (Gal. 5:6). Authentic faith comes forth in action that
concretely expresses reconciliation and transformation. "Works do
not a good man make, but a good man does good works," said
Martin Luther. "We are God's workmanship, created in Christ Jesus to do good works" (Eph. 2:10), Paul wrote to the Ephesians.

Many Christians have battled the despair that comes from attempting to work their way into God's favor. Before encountering
the God of grace, Martin Luther struggled under the tyranny of despair. Then, through his study of the Scripture, Luther came to see
that we are reconciled to God by the gracious act of God alone, that
is, by grace through faith. Now Luther understood that because of
grace, a Christian is a *perfectly free lord of all, subject to none*. Everything pertaining to salvation has been given to us by Christ. Nothing can be added to the supreme gift, and nothing in this world
can alter our relationship with God. In that sense the Christian is
"lord of all." And yet the Christian is a *dutiful servant of all, subject
to every one*, Luther added.[5] With the first part of Christian freedom
firmly in place, the second follows. Free *from* works (as a means for
salvation), a Christian is now free *for* works as expressions of love
for God and one's neighbor. Reconciled to God by grace alone and
set free from a wrong relationship to the Law, the Christian's greatest desire is to honor the Gift Giver.

Now for the first time, one can walk freely in the way of the
Lord as an expression of worship! The command to love your
neighbor as yourself can become a reality. This is the glorious

Christian freedom the apostle Paul celebrates in epistle after epistle.

The Beginning of Sanctification

The new birth or new creation accomplished by the Holy Spirit is often referred to as initial sanctification. It could even be called inaugural sanctification. It is the active work of the Spirit that actually claims us as instruments of service to God. We become "holy unto the Lord." "Now that you have been set free from sin and have become slaves to God," Paul told the Romans, "the benefit you reap leads to holiness, and the result is eternal life" (Rom. 6:22). If there were such a word, we could say that the Spirit "holifies" those in whom He is creatively working.

In the new birth, the holy God begins a richly comprehensive process aimed at bringing the whole of a person's life into conformity with Christ. Carefully and intentionally, God molds a people who manifest the way of the Lord and glorify His name. As an expression of thanksgiving for this continuing grace, Paul calls upon the Roman Christians to join him in worship by presenting themselves for sanctification: "I appeal to you therefore, brothers and sisters, by the mercies of God, to present your bodies as a living sacrifice, holy and acceptable to God, which is your spiritual worship. Do not be conformed to this world, but be transformed by the renewing of your minds, so that you may discern what is the will of God—what is good and acceptable and perfect" (Rom. 12:1-2, NRSV). Perhaps Paul best summarizes the character and goal of the sanctification process with these words: "For from him and through him and to him are all things. To him be the glory forever! Amen" (11:36, NIV).

Christian holiness has everything to do with the worship of God and love for all that is good, peaceable, just, and merciful. It is faith that works through love. It builds up the Body of Christ and manifests the name of the Lord in all the world. And although sanctification includes the individual profoundly and comprehen-

Christian holiness always travels in the company of grace, hope, and love.

sively, it has absolutely nothing to do with isolated, legalistic "piety." Christian holiness always travels in the company of grace, hope, and love, and in the direction of the kingdom of God.

Let us conclude by making sure that our center is still in focus. The kingdom of God is a kingdom of grace. Knowing that God is universally gracious is good news for anyone willing to abandon all boasts before God. The story God tells of himself in the New Testament is unmistakably clear. Anyone can join the story. In the most important sense, everyone enters the story at the same place. Better yet, God begins to retell the story of himself in those who receive the kingdom of grace.

And what a story! Without end, without measure, God invests in His children the riches of His grace. Though Paul had seen deeply into the grace of God and had scaled breathtaking heights of understanding, he told the Philippians that there were dimensions of the gospel he had only begun to explore. Nevertheless, he said, "I am consumed by a desire to move forward." (See Phil. 3:8-16.)

But what is entire sanctification? . . . it means perfect love. It is love excluding sin, love filling the heart, taking up the whole capacity of the soul. It is love "rejoicing ever more, praying without ceasing, in everything giving thanks."

—John Wesley
Sermon: "The Scripture
Way of Salvation"

For John Wesley, the doctrine of Christian holiness was yet another way of celebrating the sovereignty *of grace.*

—Albert Outler
John Wesley

We have said that the end of regeneration is that the life of believers may exhibit a symmetry and agreement between the righteousness of God and their obedience; and that thus they may confirm the adoption by which they are accepted as his children.

—John Calvin
*Institutes of the Christian
Religion,* III. vi. 1

I believe that thou art stronger than sin, and that thou canst keep me, even me. . . . So now I will trust thee. I give myself to thee. I keep back no reserves. Body, soul, and spirit, I present myself to thee as a piece of clay, to be fashioned into anything thy love and thy wisdom shall choose.

—Hannah Whitall Smith
The Christian's Secret of a Happy Life

CHAPTER 7

The Kiss

THEY CALLED HIM LIGHTNIN'—LIGHTNIN' AMMONS. HE was arguably the best shortstop ever to play for a major southeastern university. He had great hands. He turned double plays so fast that the locals called his moves greased lightnin'. Hence his name. Upon graduation, a lucrative professional career awaited Paul "Lightnin'" Ammons.

Ever since his teen years, though, Lightnin' had felt pulled in a different direction. You see, his younger brother was a Down syndrome child. So with professional scouts pointing out to Paul and his parents what a terrible error he was making, Lightnin' turned his back on a lucrative pro contract. He became a special education teacher in a small southeastern town. Annual salary? Fourteen thousand dollars. Lightnin' is still there today. Baseball? He coaches a Little League team. Regrets? "Years ago I closed one door and opened another," he says. "I would do the same thing again. I have no regrets." His action was *deliberate* and *decisive*.

Comprehensive Claims

When by grace we enter the kingdom of God, one door opens to us, and another closes. Through the gracious work of the Holy Spirit, we enter a world where obedience and transformation become characteristic of our existence. We step into a new realm of values. Through the power of the Spirit we close the door to rebellion and alienation from God. We no longer strive to build kingdoms of our own. Instead, we place ourselves under the rule of God. We begin the journey of a lifetime.

71

When Jesus calls people to discipleship, He never practices the sales gimmick known as bait and switch. There are no hidden clauses in small print. Instead, large letters declare, "Before you choose to enter the Kingdom, count the cost." *Make no mistake*, He warns. *If you want to follow me, then shoulder your cross. The old self won't be coming back alive.* (See Luke 14:27.) Jesus' language is at first perplexing: "He who finds his life will lose it, and he who loses his life for my sake will find it" (Matt. 10:39, RSV).

> *When Jesus calls people to discipleship, He never practices the sales gimmick known as bait and switch.*

What kinds of demands were these to make when great multitudes were flocking around? Jesus' support declined dramatically afterward. Apparently He hadn't hired a pollster. By using more permissive language, perhaps Jesus could have retained broad public appeal. Some would accuse Him of not knowing how to hold a crowd. Clearly, that was not His interest.

No one who follows Jesus can ever legitimately say, "You didn't tell me discipleship would be this demanding. All I ever wanted were some of the amenities." In the kingdom of God, our subjective interests do not reign. When we enter the kingdom of grace, the door to all values and pursuits that oppose God's holiness and love closes. The door to worship, obedience, and freedom opens. Let no one think otherwise about the kingdom of God.

Comprehensive Promises

Let's consider an astonishing paradox. The New Testament teaches that even those who have been in the Kingdom for a long time have to revisit its meaning over and over. Jesus demonstrated that the call to lose one's self and to be crucified with Him is in reality a call to freedom and a promise of life. This paradox lodges at the center of what it means to be a Christian. The same Christ who said, "Take up your cross," also promised, "If the Son sets you free, you will be free indeed" (John 8:36). Could anything be stranger? The kingdom of grace joins death and life, servanthood and freedom. This is the wisdom of God, which is unqualified foolishness to those in the kingdom of darkness.

Sanctification is one New Testament term for this paradoxical wisdom of the kingdom of grace ("the manifold wisdom of God" [Eph. 3:10]). It is all about dying and living. It is all about servant-hood and freedom—ever-expanding freedom. Sanctification is all about being children of the Heavenly Father. It is about citizenship in the kingdom of grace. The call to disciple-ship includes the entire range of human existence. Leaving any part of life out-side the Kingdom's domain is unthink-able.

Just what is this freedom Jesus promises?

Just what is this freedom Jesus promises? It sounds so unlike the bur-densome "discipleship" some endure. Many Christians have spent their lifetimes exploring the riches of Christian freedom and have by the end reached some of the first mile markers. On this journey they discover that Christian freedom is more than *freedom from* the tyranny of sin. (In fact, the better we understand the meaning of grace, the freer we are to confess our sins.) More important, they begin to see that Christian freedom is *freedom for* God. Because of grace, we are set free to explore the intense mutual commitment between God and humanity. We can enjoy the intimacy of an ever-deepening relationship. As a result, we begin to see God different-ly. We begin to understand how freely and creatively He has acted on our behalf.

As astonishing as the language may appear, the New Testa-ment says that Jesus Christ is the Head of a new humanity. This new humanity will be lived out in the world and as a part of the new community—the Church, the Body of Christ (Eph. 3:8-12; 4:1-7; 5:25-33). Christ is the new Adam, the Fountain of new possibili-ties through grace, the Giver of abundant life (1 Cor. 15:45). Paul's formula for describing the new humanity is this: human life lived no longer *according to the flesh* (the created order), but *in the flesh* (Gal. 2:20) and *according to (or by) the Spirit* (see Rom. 8:1-17).

The goal of the gospel is not to return us to the first Adam but to introduce us to the new Adam, Christ, our elder Brother. When we enter the kingdom of God we enter a new humanity whose Author is Jesus Christ. When Paul instructs the Roman Christians regarding the new humanity, he says that it is the "free gift" of Christ. Moreover, the new humanity proceeds from an "abundance of grace" to the glory of God. The new humanity, Paul adds, is the reign of grace in human life "by the grace of the one man, Jesus Christ" (Rom. 5:15). *This is what the New Testament means by sanctification — the comprehensive reign of grace — nothing more, nothing less.*

Life and freedom. This is what Jesus offers. Does He promise too much?

Through Christ's indwelling presence, a person in the kingdom of grace becomes fully human (a glorious state as God designed it) in the image of Christ (Rom. 8:29). When the apostle Paul discusses Christian freedom with the Corinthian Christians, he says it means *personhood being transformed in the likeness of Christ*, "from one degree of glory to another" (2 Cor. 3:18, NRSV). It is personhood under construction amid the wear and tear of life. The Contractor for this ongoing construction job is the Holy Spirit.

We cannot speak of freedom, true humanity, or personhood the way God intended it apart from Christ and the history of God's dealings with humanity. All attempts to achieve freedom and human wholeness apart from Christ are in error. So Christian life and freedom involve an unending process in which all dimensions of life are subject to the transforming reign of God. Stepping through the door of the Kingdom, we join a story that will be authored by the Holy Spirit, told in and through us (see 2 Cor. 3:3). The story will make all-inclusive claims upon us. Following our own *way* ceases to be our controlling interest. Learning His way—*the way of freedom*—will now occupy life's center. The skills of grace must be learned and practiced. We must acquire a whole new grammar of life. We must speak a whole new language. Life must now be shaped according to a new reality—the kingdom of God. Any model for Christian discipleship that yields less than this is fraudulent.

A new humanity. Life and freedom. This is what Jesus offers. Does He promise too much? Is the promise splendid but finally unrealistic? Can a person in fact truly obey Jesus' command to love God and neighbor? Can a person live freely by God's grace even in the complex and often tragic circumstances of life? Or, in order to achieve such freedom, must we abandon the plane of everyday human existence and deny our humanity? Surely any meaningful promise of freedom must take into full account our rearing children, making sometimes difficult and less-than-perfect moral decisions, fighting debilitating diseases, and paying taxes and union dues. Otherwise, the promise of Christian freedom is empty. It doesn't make contact with what we know about ourselves and the fast-paced worlds we inhabit. Simply put, does the New Testament's promise of a new humanity square with the wear-and-tear life of the real world?

When life is faced honestly, what happens to the promise? What happens to the New Testament talk about sanctification? Can love for God and neighbor really become the controlling and defining disposition of life now?

Jesus says, "Yes!" The New Testament emphasizes God's possibilities rather than humanity's incapacities, God's promises rather than humanity's fears, God's victorious presence *here* and *now* in the Holy Spirit for guidance, comfort, and strength.[1] Many others say, "No!" Unfortunately, some persons believe the power and complexity of sin, in addition to human impotence, are more formidable than the power of God's grace.

In *The Brothers Karamazov,* the 19th-century Russian novelist Dostoyevsky tells about a person named the Grand Inquisitor who answered *no.* The story of the Grand Inquisitor occurs in 15th-century Seville, Spain, during the Spanish Inquisition, when "heretics" were burned every day "to the glory of God." The Grand Inquisitor, a cardinal, conducted the Inquisition in Seville.

One day a stranger appears in the city square where heretics are burned. "He came softly, unobserved, and strange to say, every one recognized Him. The people are irresistibly drawn to Him, they surround Him, they flock about Him and follow Him. He moves silently in their midst with a gentle smile of infinite compassion. The sun of love burns in His heart, light and power shine from His eyes." Then the Grand Inquisitor passes by, sees Him, recognizes Him as Christ, and bids his guards take Him away to the gloomy, vaulted prison of the Holy Inquisition.

Later the Grand Inquisitor comes to the prison, stands for a moment or two, and gazes into Jesus' face. "Is it Thou?" he asks. "Why art Thou come to hinder us?" The Inquisitor says that Jesus misled people by telling them they could live as God's free partners. "For fifteen centuries we have been wrestling with Thy freedom, but now it is ended and over for good.

"The people," said the Inquisitor, "have brought their freedom to us and laid it humbly at our feet. . . . Men in their simplicity and their natural unruliness cannot even understand freedom. They fear it and dread it—for nothing has ever been more insupportable for a person and a human society than freedom.

"Go, and come no more," the Inquisitor told Jesus. "Come not at all, never, never!" But before Jesus left, "He suddenly approached the old man in silence and kissed him on his bloodless aged lips. That was all He answered. The old man shuddered."

What happened to the Inquisitor? "The kiss glows in his heart, but the old man adheres to his idea."[2]

Are there dimensions of life that have to remain outside the kingdom of God?

Some Christians are like the Inquisitor. For all their good intentions, they doubt that Christ can set them free. And even though they have been kissed by Him, they persist in their denial. They fail to see that having been re-created by Christ, they are free to live "according to the Spirit" (Rom. 8:1-8).

Dostoyevsky challenges us to consider whose estimate of what Christ can accomplish in His disciples is the correct one. Jesus declares that God can so transform a person that he or she can live freely and confidently in the stream of grace (John 7:37-39). He teaches that a disciple can love God so comprehensively, and know the Spirit's empowerment so deeply, that the new humanity can in fact spread to the whole of life. Or—is the Grand Inquisitor correct? Must life in the Kingdom be forever marginal, fearful, and infantile? Must it be forever crippled by cycles of victory and defeat? Are there dimensions of life that have to remain outside the kingdom of God?

The most normal aspiration of a young pine tree is to reach for the golden sun. The normal aspiration of a child of God in whom the Spirit dwells should be that the defining center of his or her life be characterized by love for God and all that God loves. "Just as you once yielded your members to impurity . . ." Paul told the Roman Christians, "so now yield your members to righteousness for sanctification" (6:19, RSV). The Gospels and Epistles of the New Testament consistently describe such yielding as not limited to an order of supersaints, but as the norm for every day Christian life. It is simply the unfolding of Kingdom life in the child of God and within the Body of Christ.

The kingdom of grace does not limit its designs in any area of life, and the child of God should long for nothing less. The sovereignty of grace is demonstrated in the comprehensiveness of its reach. "Let the peace of Christ *rule* in your hearts," Paul wrote to the Colossians. "Let the word of Christ dwell in you *richly*" (3:15-16, emphasis added). Paul's desire for these Christians was that God's love would so characterize them that it would *harmonize* the whole of life. The comprehensive reign of God is simply another way of talking about the kingdom of God, which was inaugurated in Jesus Christ and which we enter by grace through faith.

Comprehensive Provision

The New Testament teaches that the kingdom of grace can comprehensively reign in God's children. Consistently, the writers use terms such as wholeness, completeness, thoroughness, and soundness to describe the reign of grace in the life of a Christian. One excellent illustration occurs in Paul's first letter to the Thessalonian Christians. The apostle prayed that "the God of peace" would "sanctify [them] *wholly*" (5:23, RSV, emphasis added). He then adds, "And may your *spirit* and *soul* and *body* be kept sound and blameless at the coming of our Lord Jesus Christ" (v. 23, RSV, emphasis added). The whole person for the kingdom of grace. Quite unlike the Grand Inquisitor, Paul was confident that the God who calls us to wholeness can accomplish it (v. 24).

"Sanctify you wholly." Breathtaking language! Breathtaking promises! Breathtaking Kingdom! We know that God alone is holy. We've seen in chapter 1 that the word can be used with reference to the creation only when some aspect of that creation is claimed as a special instrument for declaring the glory of God, for making known His name and His *way*. Sanctification resides at the center of the kingdom of grace. Sanctification is the *process of making holy*. To be *wholly* or *entirely* sanctified means that we place our whole existence at the disposal of the Kingdom. It involves the Holy Spirit cleansing us from any lingering obstruction to Christ's Lordship and empowering us for victorious living and service. The term *sanctification* communicates a point of departure as well as a destination. It means placing *all* of life in the stream of transforming grace.

Real sanctification has nothing to do with isolated, introverted, and neurotic piety.

As we have noted all along, the principal purpose of all that God does in and through us is to declare or reveal himself. Real sanctification has nothing to do with isolated, introverted, and neurotic piety. Instead, it has everything to do with an all-consuming enthusiasm for God's disclosure of himself and His purposes for creation. Sanctification harnesses *all* dimensions of life for service to righteousness, mercy, justice, and love. This is the meaning of Christian wholeness. Donald Bloesch has captured this in one succinct statement: "Being a holy God He is satisfied with nothing less than holiness in all manner of conduct (cf. Lev. 11:44; 19:2; Isa. 52:11). Being a loving God He strives to instill His love in the people He has created and called to service in His Kingdom."[3]

Comprehensively placing oneself in the service of grace is both a deliberate and decisive action. This sanctification can occur whenever the Holy Spirit reveals to a disciple of Christ just how thorough the claims of the kingdom of grace really are. It happens when a child of God confronts the fact that from the center of his or her being, to the outer reaches of life, Christ must be Lord of all.

There is no single or stereotypical experiential mode through which we are sanctified. There is no single form of experience through which the Spirit works. The free Spirit of God works as He pleases (John 3:6-8; 2 Cor. 3:17). Consciously and completely embracing the Lordship of Christ may occur early in one's discipleship or later. It may occur dramatically or over an extended period of time. It may be a quiet dawning awareness or more climactic. The way in which the Spirit wholly establishes Christ's Lordship is incidental. The substance is essential. John Wesley said that in all instances when we are considering the work of God in His children, we should carefully avoid "limiting the Almighty. He doeth whatsoever and whensoever it pleaseth him. He can convey his grace" in any manner in which "his free spirit is pleased most to work in our hearts."[4]

Whatever the Holy Spirit's preparatory process, there is a time when by grace and through faith disciples of Jesus open themselves to the Spirit's sanctifying presence, just as one does in justification. This is an essential dimension of the Good News. At this juncture He crowns every dimension of the human spirit with love for God and neighbor, and Christ claims us comprehensively for His own. In a love that is equally decisive and extensive, we open the whole of our lives to the Spirit's sanctifying activity. From there, John Wesley said, we go on in a love for God and neighbor that "increases more and more."[5]

Not surprisingly, the Holy Spirit works with respect for our individual histories.

Not surprisingly, the Holy Spirit works with respect for our individual histories. Each of us has a different personality type, domestic background, religious history, and so on. A good craftsman takes seriously the material with which he or she works. The finished work of art will show the artist's skill and ability to respect, maintain, and develop the integrity of the medium, whether it be wood, stone, clay, or paint. The Carpenter from Nazareth is just such a craftsman.

Christians use a rich treasure of phrases to describe the Holy Spirit's work in bringing the child of God to embrace comprehensively Christ's Lordship: "the deeper life," "the fullness of the Spirit," "entire sanctification," "love made perfect," "Christian holiness," "Christian perfection." All these phrases are means of describing the reign of grace. All of them identify a decisive advance in understanding and in embracing the all-inclusive claims of Christ as Lord of all.

Each term bespeaks the Holy Spirit's faithfulness to us in revealing the riches, promises, and reaches of God's grace. When speaking of "the fullness of the Spirit," we mean that the Holy Spirit is now free to administer in us all the gifts of grace Christ's atonement secured for us. From the center of our being outward, the Spirit of Christ is free to establish His reign.

Because of the Spirit's empowerment, the Christian life doesn't have to be a struggle. *Entire sanctification* means that through the Spirit's work in us, all dimensions of life are open to transformation by Him. *Love made perfect* means that love for God and neighbor is made the central and defining disposition (or

. . . when speaking of sanctification, some Christians claim too much.

bent) of our lives. Taking on the disposition of Christ certainly does not imply anything so foolish as always loving perfectly or being sinless. Only of God is this true. *Christian holiness* means that provisionally the One who is the image of the holy God is now free without restriction to re-create His image in us. We are vessels committed to His holy purposes. *Christian perfection* can be a sticky and misleading term. But it need not be. It simply and beautifully means that what God has *designed* (purposed) for us as Christians who live in the world, and what Christ died to *secure* for us, the Holy Spirit can now *accomplish* in us. It is simply another way of celebrating and living out the reign of grace in every part of life. The phrase should not be distorted to mean "perfectionism," "flawlessness," or "sinlessness." In a spirit of celebration, the apostle announced that although sin once reigned over us, now grace will "reign through righteousness to eternal life through Jesus Christ our Lord" (Rom. 5:21, RSV).

The sanctifying work of the Holy Spirit can be misjudged in at least two ways. On the one hand, some Christians hope for, or ex-

pect, too little. They do not believe that the Holy Spirit can empower the Christian to live with love for God and one's neighbor
as the defining disposition of life. On the other hand, when speaking of sanctification, some Christians claim too much. They forget
that we now live between the *already* and the *not yet* of the kingdom of God. The Kingdom *has already been inaugurated,* but it certainly has *not yet been consummated.* The first error depreciates the
significance of the *already.* The second error ignores the importance
of the *not yet.* The first error can breed carelessness, laziness, and
superficiality. The second error can breed arrogance, dishonesty,
and frustration. The Christian doctrine of sanctification requires a
sturdy balance between the *already* and the *not yet.* By God's grace
and the Spirit's empowerment, we live *from* the Kingdom's inauguration and journey *toward* its fulfillment. Sanctification includes
both the Spirit's present accomplishment and His ongoing work.
So fulfilling "the high calling of God in Christ Jesus" (Phil. 3:14,
KJV) is both *already* and *not yet.* Between the two lies a lifetime of
maturation and confession.

Wholeness is a *present reality*—every dimension of life is to be
surrendered to transformation by the Spirit. Wholeness is also a
state of anticipation—watching for what the Spirit will continue to
do until the Kingdom comes in its fullness. When we live in the
fullness of the Spirit, we submit all of life to divine creativity. We
are not hung up on "perfectionism." We walk in grace, humility,
and faith as we mature in our journey. We do not exhibit arrogance, self-satisfaction, and arrested growth.

One beautiful account of someone decisively embracing
Christ's comprehensive Lordship comes from the life of Lloyd
Ogilvie, for many years the pastor of the Hollywood, California,
First Presbyterian Church and now chaplain of the United States
Senate. He says:

I'll never forget it as long as I live. After completing my
postgraduate work, I began my work as a Presbyterian pastor.
I was washed, starched, and almost insulated from any authentic power from on high. I was more concerned about the
robes I wore than about being fully clothed with the Holy
Spirit, more concerned about my collar than my Bible. And
nothing was happening in my church.

I decided I would either leave the ministry, or I would receive the fullness of the Holy Spirit that Jesus described in the 14th-16th chapters of John. I went away for the summer. I took my Bible with me and nothing else. I can still remember it. A long, lonely beach. I walked and talked with the Lord. I talked and I prayed for a whole month.

On the day before I was to leave, on the beach, in the sand, I took a stick and wrote all the things that were standing in the way of the total Lordship of Christ in my life. My insecurities, fears, frustrations, the devices of human manipulation of people, my longing for power, for recognition, my pride, arrogance—I wrote it in the sand.

Then I got on my knees, and Jesus repeated in my soul what he had told his disciples: "Apart from me you can do nothing." There, while I was on my knees, Jesus fulfilled his promise: "Abide in me and I in you." An electric current began at the top of my head and moved to the soles of my feet. The power of Christ, the abiding Spirit, transformed my life. I moved from knowledge of my own education to the gift of knowledge, from my own insight to God's wisdom.

> *Let me no more my comfort draw,*
> *from my frail grasp on Thee.*
> *In this alone my only awe,*
> *Thy mighty grasp on me!*

Dr. Ogilvie would never impose the form of his experience with the Holy Spirit on anyone. His account is as unique as the creative touch of the Holy Spirit can make it. But he does urge upon us all a total surrender to Christ as the center of one's life, and a commitment to allow the unhampered freedom of the Holy Spirit to govern and empower us.

> *Now to him who by the power at work within us is able to accomplish abundantly far more than all we can ask or imagine, to him be glory in the church and in Christ Jesus to all generations, forever and ever. Amen* (Eph. 3:20-21, NRSV).

We believe in the Church, the community that confesses Jesus Christ as Lord, the covenant people of God made new in Christ, the Body of Christ called together by the Holy Spirit through the Word.

—Articles of Faith, XI
Manual, Church of the Nazarene

———

One can only know what the Church should be now if one also knows what the Church was originally.

—Hans Kung
The Church

———

Christianity is essentially a social religion. . . . To turn it into a solitary one is to destroy it. . . . The Gospel of Christ knows . . . no holiness but social holiness.

—John Wesley
The Works of John Wesley, 5:296, 302
Poetical Works, 1:xxii

———

Private Christianity is not Christianity at all.

—Karl Barth
The Humanity of God

———

Christianity means community through Jesus Christ and in Jesus Christ.

—Dietrich Bonhoeffer
Life Together

CHAPTER 8

More than the Members

WHEN FLASHING YELLOW LIGHTS APPEAR AS WE AP-
proach an intersection, we immediately prepare to alter the way
we've been driving. We slow down. We watch carefully for further
instructions or prepare for a change of direction.

Caution lights greet us as we enter this chapter. They signal
that we should read carefully and be prepared to make some important shifts. Together we will consider carefully how the New
Testament presents the Church. By *Church,* we don't mean denominations or buildings, but the Universal Body of Christ in which all
who dwell in Christ have their life. Denominations can serve the
Church, but they must never be equated with it.

This chapter is important because of an essential relationship
between the holy life and life in the Body of Christ. For the New
Testament writers, holy living is as inseparable from the Church as
the wings of a jumbo jet are inseparable from its fuselage. In our
day the Church is often relegated to a secondary role when people
define the holy life. In the New Testament, things are quite different. There, as we'll see, holy living and the Church form a comple-
mentary unity that cannot be dissolved.

As you read, be prepared for some sharp turns and challenges.
We will ask you to think in some ways that are out of step with the
20th century. Of course, the New Testament, not the 20th century,
should shape our life in the Body of Christ. We want our thinking
to be formed by the New Testament's picture of the relationship
between the Church and holy living. At points, the thrust of this
chapter might be compared to asking someone who believes the

earth is flat to think of the earth as round. The differences between the New Testament and the 20th century are just about that great. So hold on.

Paradigm Shift

As the Middle Ages closed and the modern era (1400s-1500s) began to dawn, a major change occurred in how we think of persons in relationship to society. This change also affected how we think about science, work, and government. The change significantly influences how most of us view the Church.[1]

The New Testament teaches that the Church is the primary context in which we learn to live the holy life. In the community of grace we learn to practice the reign of Christ and anticipate the Kingdom's consummation. Only through the Body of Christ do we "share in the inheritance of the saints" for which the Father has qualified us (Col. 1:12). Here in the Church, says ethicist Stanley Hauerwas, we learn to live according to Christian convictions.[2]

> *The New Testament teaches that the Church is the primary context in which we learn to live the holy life.*

Before the Renaissance, individual persons were perceived and valued principally with reference to the institutions with which they were connected. Persons gained their identity in relationship to larger wholes such as people groups, guilds, nation-states, and the Church. When thinking of the individual, one did not begin with the individual and then work toward a larger social group such as family or nation. Instead, one began with the larger corporate social entity and then moved to the smaller unit, the individual. The larger social whole or institution was thought to be more real and important than the individual. Individuals simply didn't have the significance we assign to them today. Don't be surprised if this is difficult to comprehend—it is quite different from the way we think today.

Toward the end of the Middle Ages this way of thinking slowly began to change, and perceptions reversed. Gradually, the individual emerged as having primary importance, and institutions and traditions assumed a secondary role. A good example of the shift is seen in society's approach to the sciences. Consider the way our culture encourages young scientists to think in new ways and to develop groundbreaking experiments in the treatment of cancer. Their research will likely challenge ideas about cancer held on to for a long time by the scientific establishment. Before the modern era, the curiosity of the young scientists would have been quite naturally surrendered to orthodox tradition. The experiments would not have occurred.

Earth is not the center of the universe after all, Copernicus had discovered.

Today individuals hold the importance and primary rank once assigned to institutions. We begin with the human ego as the first reality and build from there. Characteristically, institutions have only the significance the human ego grants. Without this big change in perspective, modernity as we have known it could not have occurred.[3]

As we would expect, shifting the focus to the individual had a profound influence on human life and thought. For one thing, it made modern science possible. Because of the new prominence of individuals, scientists turned away from the authority of philosophical and ecclesiastical traditions and looked to the world—to particular existing things—for answers to their questions. In the 1500s, for instance, Nicolaus Copernicus examined the universe and decided that Ptolemy, the second-century Egyptian astronomer, had been wrong. Earth is not the center of the universe after all, Copernicus had discovered.

In many ways all of us have benefited from the modern turn to the individual. But individualism can become too extreme. It can overwhelm social responsibility and any sense of belonging to a larger whole. Western society is now in decline, partly because of extreme individualism. Consider the impact the current preoccupation with "individual happiness" is having on the nuclear family. The notion is now popular that a husband or wife can dissolve a marriage if either of them is not being "individually fulfilled."

Harvard professor Michael Sandel has discussed this crisis in *Democracy's Discontent*. In an atmosphere of runaway individualism, he says, everything is framed in terms of personal rights, autonomy, privacy, and choice. The search for the good has yielded to the search for rights. We see this self-centeredness daily in professional sports, politics, the entertainment industry, and so on.[4]

The Modern Influence

In profound ways, the shift to thinking of individuals as having primary importance has also affected how we view the Church. Now, in the Western world at least, the Church is thought of largely from the perspective of modern individualism. Christians *as individuals* have come to hold the place of primary significance when deciding the nature and importance of the Church. Should we be surprised to learn that this is not the way the New Testament presents the Body of Christ and its members?

When we discover major discrepancies in the way we view the Church and the way Scripture regards it, the New Testament must prevail. One reason is that the New Testament's view of the Church offers a much richer understanding of Christ's Body and Christian discipleship than modern individualism can provide. Only the way of Scripture can fully open to us Christ's riches of community and redemption. Since most of us are more deeply affected by the modern way of thinking than we might realize, accepting correction by the New Testament might not be easy.

There are at least three ways modern individualism has drawn many of us away from the New Testament picture of the Church. First we will note the influences, and then we will return to examine the influences in light of the New Testament.

. . . individual Christians are neither the Church's source nor its life.

1. Today it is common practice for Christians to say, or to imply, that individual Christians, taken as a group, are the Church's origin. Individual Christians create the Church by voluntarily forming themselves into congregations. And when all the Christians in the world are taken together, the universal Church results, much

as a wall results from the required number of concrete blocks. Members of an adult Sunday School class were asked, "Who creates the Church?" Almost in unison, and without a dissenting voice, they responded, "We do!" Based squarely on their modern individualism, they thought of the Church as something that results from a voluntary association of individual Christians whom the Lord crowns with His presence when they gather. For the Christians in the Sunday School class, the Church's origin is comparable to the origin of a quilting club or a car pool.

Wrong. The New Testament teaches that the Father creates the Church through the Son (1 Cor. 1:9) and by the Holy Spirit. In one important sense, Christians do compose the Body of Christ. But according to the New Testament, individual Christians are neither the Church's source nor its life.

2. Today many Christians think that the Church is *no more* than the sum of its individual parts. We speak as though "Church" is simply the name for all the Christians taken as a whole. As such, it is just like any other assembled entity. An automobile is what one has when the individual parts are in place and functioning properly. But the automobile is no more than that—just a correct association of related parts. The same could be said of televisions and dishwashers.

Automobiles, televisions, and dishwashers fail completely as illustrations for explaining the New Testament's picture of the Church. As we will see, the Church is far more than the sum of its parts.

3. Today Christians think that God redeems us primarily *as individuals,* and that our redemption is only secondarily, or incidentally, related to the Church. Christians, as the modern understanding of salvation goes, are joined to Christ principally as private, self-contained individuals. Salvation is like an exclusive two-party contract. God has made identical contracts with others. We might discuss our contract with others and even receive a better understanding of it, but the contract as such is unaffected by others. Rather than use the human body (in which each part is interdependent) as a metaphor for the Church as Paul did, our prevailing view of salvation is better illustrated by a series of individually sealed cables feeding into a computer.

The trail of these three modern ways of thinking about the Church is not at all difficult to find. It leads back directly to the big change at the beginning of the modern era. Most of us have inherited its influence without giving it much thought. We may even be surprised to learn that our ancient Christian brothers and sisters thought differently about the Church and would be quite puzzled by a conversation with us.

So what? Maybe the early Christians thought of the Church in one way, and we in another. Perhaps the difference is not important. When one drives from St. Louis to Chicago, whether the driver believes the earth is flat or round will make no difference. Getting to Chicago is the only important thing.

Paul's "Letter to the Moderns"

The apostle Paul, among other New Testament writers, would not agree on the legitimacy of our analogy. He spoke explicitly regarding the nature of the Church. He would be astonished to learn of the modern influences we have just named. He would probably have written at least one "Letter to the Moderns." What would he likely have said?

After an introduction in which Paul identified himself as a servant of Jesus Christ, and an apostle set apart for the gospel of God, he would greet us in the name of Jesus Christ. He would probably commend to us the grace and peace of God our Father and the Lord Jesus Christ. Before the letter had proceeded very far, Paul would begin to address the three marks of modernity that appear in our speech. We would quickly discover that Paul's perception of the Church (*ecclesia*, i.e., "congregation," "community") differs significantly from ours.

The Church should not be compared with the Kiwanis Club or Rotary Club.

First of all, Paul would likely address our modern notion that Christians, by their voluntary associations, *create* the Church. He certainly spoke of Christians as members of Christ's Body, and in that sense they *compose* the Church. But they do not *create* the Church. Paul would teach us that the Church is *created* by God through

Christ and by the work of the Holy Spirit. Paul told the Corinthian Christians that just as each part of the human body makes its contribution to the whole, even so the members of Christ's Body have diverse gifts through which they enrich each other. However, God is the One who grants the gifts and *activates* the members of Christ's Body. "To each is given the manifestation of the Spirit for the common good" (1 Cor. 12:7, NRSV).

If Paul is correct, then the Church should not be compared with the Kiwanis Club or Rotary Club. Both of these service organizations arose through the initiative of persons of goodwill who shared interests in common. Many of their members also share similar social and economic identifications. But human effort could never have created such a diverse bunch as we find in the Church.

Membership in the Body of Christ rests completely on grace.

Speaking of "bunch," this is a good word picture for the Church. Jesus taught that the Church stands in relationship to himself as branches and grapes do to a grapevine (John 15:1-8). We might say that churches are like bunches of grapes, drawing life from Christ. He, the Vine, is the Church's origin and life (John 15:16). Just as bunches of grapes depend upon the vine, Paul would tell us that the Church is a living reality *only* because it constantly receives life from its Source, not because it has any resources of its own.

We might inform Paul that we moderns believe that individual citizens create the civil state. But he would ask us how we came to think of the Church as originating in the same way. What applies to the secular state does not apply to the Church. Unlike the state, the Church is constituted by Christ's life, death, resurrection, and by Pentecost. The Church is the dominion of Christ on earth. It is the continuing work of the exalted Lord, created by Him through the Holy Spirit.

Through the centuries, Christians have turned to Jesus' high-priestly prayer in John 17 to help them understand the origins and meaning of the Church. In this passage Jesus prays first for himself

(vv. 1-5), then for the disciples (6-19), and finally for the Church universal (20-26). In verse 23 Jesus states the Church's constitution, its essence: "I in them, and thou in me" (KJV). Clearly, Jesus' words dispel the notion that the Church is a human creation. Instead, the Church stands forth by the will of the Father as expressed in His Son.

Throughout the New Testament, we see this theme reinforced. Christ has called the Church into being through the Holy Spirit and by the will of the Father. He is its Savior, and to Him it is subject (Eph. 5:23-24). The Church is "the fellowship of his Son, Jesus Christ our Lord" (1 Cor. 1:9, NRSV). It is the new community (*koinonia*, i.e., "fellowship") of grace gathered in Christ by the will of the Father. The Church is the

The Church is not like an automobile or dishwasher, whose substance doesn't rise above the totality of its parts.

Bride of Christ (Rev. 21:9), the new wineskin (Matt. 9:17), the holy temple of the Lord (Eph. 2:20-21), and the Body of Christ (Eph. 5:23). He is its Head (Col. 1:18).

As a divine creation, the Church is the community of grace and faith. Just as reconciliation with God comes by grace through faith, so the Church of Jesus Christ has God's grace as its sole foundation. Membership in the Body of Christ rests completely on grace. No one is a part of the fellowship because he or she wills or deserves it. If the Church were a human creation, prejudicial standards for membership would surely emerge, and the Pharisees would rule again.

Forgiveness and reconciliation with God lie at the center of the gospel. This is no less true of the Church whose members are being redeemed. The only legitimate claim to membership in Christ's Church any of us have is God's forgiveness. "The Father . . . has qualified you to share in the inheritance of the saints," Paul told the Colossians (Col. 1:12). By God's grace alone, we are now brothers and sisters in Christ. Thankfully, none of us will decide who our sisters and brothers will be.

Second, in his "Letter to the Moderns" Paul would help us understand that the Church is far *more* than just the sum of Christians gathered or scattered. The Church is not like an automobile or dishwasher, whose substance doesn't rise above the totality of its parts.

Paul's metaphor of Christ as the Head of the Church can help us grasp the difference (Eph. 4:15-16; 5:21-33; Col. 1:18). As we know quite well, a person is more than an accumulation of living organs. Each of us is characterized as a living system with a consciousness that is far more than the body—the brain included—could produce. By way of analogy, Paul tells us that as important as the individual members of the Church are, Christ the Head *is* the Church's life, its consciousness, and its uniting center. Christ has become *embodied* in the Church.

Paul says that God put His power on display in the resurrection of Jesus. Now, through Christ, the power of God that raised Jesus from the dead is at work in the Church as its life principle and central point of identity (Eph. 1:19-20). Enlivened by Christ, the members of the Church "grow up in every way into him who is the head, into Christ" (4:15, RSV).

Obviously, Christ who is the Head of the Church precedes the members of His body. The members of the Church, "joined and knit together" in love, exist in Him *who is far more than all the members combined* (Eph. 4:16, RSV).

There is an additional way for explaining how the Church is more than the sum of its parts. The Church is joined to "the kingdom of [God's] beloved Son" (Col. 1:13, RSV), which we enter through conversion. The Kingdom is God's creation, not ours. It has an objective reality that transcends its citizens. The Kingdom exists because God willed it. He expresses His reign in part through the Church. And the primary substance of the Church is not its individual members, but the God who reigns through it.

In the same way, Christians often think of the fellowship *(koinonia)* we enjoy in the Church as the result of Christian goodwill and community. Not so. The Spirit of God *is* the fellowship into which Christians are called. Put another way, the *fellowship* that constitutes the Church is the presence of the Spirit himself. The Church's *koinonia* is first of all fellowship *with* the Spirit. The oneness we experience among the sisters and the brothers is the Holy Spirit at work among us, creating a community of redemption.

So you see, the sense of community we experience in God's congregation is far different from the camaraderie we might experience at a summer office picnic or a reception for a beloved friend who is retiring. Instead, the *fellowship of the Spirit* is God's holy, redeeming presence creating a community of persons who are united in the Spirit. Mutual attraction or common interests are not the glue that holds the Church together. The glue of the Church is the grace of God that calls sinners out of darkness and places His seal upon them.

> *Mutual attraction or common interests are not the glue that holds the Church together.*

The **third** modern influence on our understanding of the Church is the tendency for people to think of themselves as individual worlds, complete unto themselves. Many things have contributed to what sociologists call the *insular* perception of the self. The word is related to *insulated* and refers to living as though one were an island.

The frenzy of urban living is one factor that made us forget how essentially related we are to other persons. The way we obtain goods and services is another. Except perhaps when some families cut their own Christmas trees at tree farms, most of us have little or no contact with those who produce the products upon which we depend. Elementary schoolteachers are sometimes amused to learn that some children don't even know the sources of cereal, bacon, or milk. We could almost say the refrigerator is our nearest and most important neighbor.

This lifestyle has directly affected our understanding of redemption. In our day, Christians commonly speak as though Christ redeems them in isolation. Supposedly, justification and sanctification occur directly and completely between God and individual Christians. But the New Testament claims that our redemption occurs essentially and inseparably in community. This concept strikes many of us as quite strange, if not objectionable. To hear that other members of the Body of Christ play an essential role in our redemption, that the life of Christian holiness occurs principally in, and draws life from, the Church sounds too much like Roman Catholicism. God redeems us as individuals, we would insist, and the Church plays only a supporting role.

"How did you reach this conclusion?" the apostle Paul might ask us. "How did you decide that God redeems us as though we were self-contained units? Do you really think that your redemption is only incidentally related to your brothers and sisters in Christ?"

Paul would agree that Christ redeems persons. All of us are identifiable individuals with particular histories and possibilities. As persons, we understand that we are subjects of God's love and restoration. Paul's letter to the Ephesians describes how God brought us into the stream of grace individually:

The Christian faith has no interest in eliminating individuality.

"But God, who is rich in mercy, out of the great love with which he loved us even when we were dead through our trespasses, made us alive together with Christ—by grace you have been saved" (Eph. 2:4-5, NRSV). The Christian faith has no interest in eliminating individuality.

But though we recognize the importance of the personal dimension of salvation, we must not ignore the importance of the *koinonia* (fellowship) in redemption. Paul addresses the Church in his letters, *not* isolated individuals who hold private contracts between themselves and God. Paul says that God "made us alive *together* with Christ" (Eph. 2:5, NRSV, emphasis added). And while individuals are important, Paul describes the glories of redemption and the call to holy living *only in relationship to the Body of Christ.* For Paul (and for Jesus, the Vine) the godly walk occurs essentially in fellowship with the Holy Spirit and with the sisters and brothers who are members of Christ's Church.

That They May All Be One

In no part of the Christian faith is there greater tension between modern culture and the New Testament. Individualism tears at the fabric of the Church and the gospel. We'll say it again—God does redeem *persons.* But for Paul, and the rest of the New Testament writers, none of us are redeemed simply as individuals. The *koinonia* of the Holy Spirit, and the brothers and sisters in that fellowship, are vital to the redemption of any single Christian. The Holy Spirit builds us up together as sisters and brothers in Christ.

The Christians in Corinth were having a difficult time understanding the importance one member has to another. For various reasons some of them wanted to go it alone. *"Wouldn't it be foolish for the eye to say to the hand, 'I really don't have any need for you. I am quite self-contained'?"* Paul asked them. (See 1 Cor. 12:21-27.) "You are the body of Christ and individually members of it" (v. 27, NRSV), he declared.

The saving and sanctifying activity of the holy God, Paul instructs the Corinthians, occurs in and through the Body of Christ. Far more than being just a figure of speech, the sisters and brothers really are "members of one another" (Eph. 4:25, NRSV; cf. Rom. 15:1-3). Through the gifts of the Spirit, the grace of God flows from one to another. We are ministers one to another, and means of grace one to another, "so that the church may be built up" (1 Cor. 14:5, NRSV).

The Epistles of Paul lead us to see that the 20th century would have a difficult time providing a model for the Church. As we study the New Testament, we realize that on the Christian journey no one travels alone. No one

As we study the New Testament, we realize that on the Christian journey no one travels alone.

knows Christ or lives the holy life in isolation. We are redeemed apart from our sisters and brothers no more than the lungs draw breath apart from the heart, or the mind interprets colors apart from the eyes.

What good news! The gospel frees us from the isolation and alienation fostered by sin. For the first time, we see other people as we ought to—from the vantage point of grace (2 Cor. 5:16). For the first time, "neighbor" as God intended it becomes a possibility. Community, patterned not after human interests and criteria but after the meaning and power of grace, becomes a reality in the *koinonia* of the Holy Spirit.

We've seen that the importance of the Church—of community—for holy living is beautifully illustrated using the human body as a metaphor. But an even higher model for Christian life in the Church is the Trinity.

In Jesus' high-priestly prayer, He uses His relationship to the Father to demonstrate our relationship one to another in the Church. In exalted language, Jesus says that the members of the Church are united one to another even as the Father and Son are reliant upon one another. "That they may all be one," He prays. "As you, Father, are in me and I am in you, may they also be in us, so that the world may believe that you have sent me" (John 17:21, NRSV).

Christians sometimes describe the Trinity as "the three-per-soned One." We sing, "God in three Persons, blessed Trinity." There is one God who is at the same time Father, Son, and Holy Spirit. The Trinity is marked by distinction without division. Each person of the Trinity has a special office or ministry. But in each office or ministry, God in His fullness is present. Take the creation, for example. We say that the Father created through the Son and by the Holy Spirit. The Church is another example. We say that the Church is the Church of God. The Father calls the Church into being through the completed work of Christ and by the enlivening Holy Spirit. Christ is our Redeemer, we confess. But we also say that the Father was redemptively at work in His Son, and that the Son rendered perfect obedience to the Father through the power of the Holy Spirit (Luke 4:1). The Book of Hebrews says that Christ offered himself up to the Father "through the eternal Spirit" (Heb. 9:14).

Throughout Scripture we see the oneness and community of the Trinity. Christ intends the same for the Church. Modern individualism can't even speak the language of the high-priestly prayer. And neither can we, unless the Holy Spirit enables us. "As you, Father, are in me and I am in you, may they also be in us, so that the world may believe that you have sent me" (John 17:21, NRSV)—so that the world may believe.

We must not miss Jesus' prayer for us. We will bear witness to Christ through our relationship to our sisters and brothers in Christ. We will bear witness to the God who is creating a community of redemption by allowing that community to be established among us. Jesus' words are clear: redemption and proclamation of the gospel cannot occur apart from love for and commitment to Christ's Church. Modern attempts to approach redemption apart from receiving life in the *koinonia* of the Holy Spirit are fundamentally misdirected.

Few records of conflict and hatred among people groups rival that between Armenians and Turks. Today the Armenians are scattered all over the earth. But between 1893 and 1896, the Turkish conquerors of Armenia killed between 20,000 and 50,000 Armenians. In 1915 the Turks drove the majority of the people of Armenia out into the Syrian Desert in order to stop them from helping the Russian army. Hundreds of thousands of Armenians died of starvation, exhaustion, and sunstroke in the desert.

On a Sunday morning in 1984 in Flushing, New York, Pastor Barry Wetstone was preaching on what it means to be a part of the Body of Christ. He was explaining Paul's statement in Ephesians 2:14-15: "For he is our peace, who has made us both one, and has broken down the dividing wall of hostility, by abolishing in his flesh the law of commandments and ordinances, that he might create in himself one new man" (RSV). On that morning the Holy Spirit moved freely in the multicultural Flushing congregation.

Barry says that at a particularly charged moment, two women stood spontaneously. One woman, Rose, was an Armenian. The other, Virginia, was Turkish. Both were Christians. The two women moved toward each other, met, embraced each other, and began to confess to each other the hostilities that had alienated them. Then, Barry says, through tears Rose and Virginia began to share with each other the peace of Christ, asking forgiveness, telling each other how the communion of the Holy Spirit was more powerful than the hatreds that had divided them.

That is the Church, the new community of grace. And that is the story of grace, hope, and holiness the Church has to tell.

There is also a repentance and a faith . . . which are requisite after we have "believed the gospel"; yea, and in every subsequent stage of our Christian course, or we cannot "run the race which is set before us." And this repentance and faith are full as necessary, in order to our continuance and growth in grace, as the former faith and repentance were, in order to our entering into the kingdom of God.

—John Wesley
Sermon: "The Repentance
of Believers"

In confession the breakthrough to community takes place.

—Dietrich Bonhoeffer
Life Together

Sin is truly sin, whether committed before or after Christ has been known, and God always hates sin.

—Martin Luther
Commentary on Galatians

CHAPTER 9

Love Story

HEAR THE PARABLE OF THE ROSE. TWO WORKERS CAME upon a single red rose beside an abandoned house. It reigned in elegance atop a long, green stem graced by many beautiful leaves.

Struck by the rose's beauty, the two workers decided to cut it and display it in their humble work shed. Having cut the rose, one worker stood holding it by the stem. "The real beauty of a rose is in its color," he said to his friend.

"Oh, no," responded the other worker. "The beauty of the rose is in its unique shape." With that, he jerked the rose from the first worker's hands.

"It's the color," insisted the first worker as he snatched back the rose.

Not to be outdone, the other worker became very angry. "It's the shape, you fool!" he yelled as he tore the rose out of the first worker's hands.

The argument increased in intensity as the rose passed roughly from one pair of hands to the other. After a while the first worker looked down to the rose he had grabbed so blindly. To his surprise he had retrieved only a bruised stem. Rose petals and leaves lay in disarray about mud-caked boots.

The gospel of the Kingdom is both rugged *and* delicate. It can disarm the powers and authorities that stand against it (Col. 2:13-15) and demolish the strongholds of Satan (2 Cor. 10:4). But it can be bruised by those who handle it too roughly. This can happen in many ways, one of which is the failure to maintain the fine balance among the gospel's interrelated parts.

Let's consider one important dimension of life in the kingdom of grace—confession of sin. Along the way we will examine two errors that damage an important part of the gospel message.

Joined at the Hip:
Two Faulty Understandings of Grace

If a person in the first century had been looking for a perfect church, he or she would have quickly skipped past the one in Corinth. The two New Testament letters written to the young church catalog numerous disruptive problems. Still, Paul addressed the Corinthians as "those sanctified in Christ Jesus, called to be saints" (1 Cor. 1:2, RSV). The Corinthian Christians were holy but were also plagued by serious problems. In fact, their church was loaded with error. They were holy because by faith they were in Christ as part of His Body. They had been called to holy living as an unending journey.

Among the problems identified in the Corinthian church were at least two fundamental errors regarding God's grace. Both mistakes occurred because one dimension of grace was emphasized and the other neglected.

The **first** error comes when we camp out on the forgiveness of sins Christ gives us. We emphasize our inability to earn God's forgiveness, and our continuing dependence upon His grace. But while the gift of forgiveness is central, sanctification is almost forgotten—the transforming work of the Holy Spirit goes begging (1 Cor. 6:12-18). And though this view stresses the freedom from guilt Christ gives, it overlooks the fact that God wants Christians to live as servants of righteousness through the indwelling Spirit (Rom. 6:15-23). It emphasizes Christ's gift of reconciliation but diminishes Christ's call to discipleship. This view correctly acknowledges that in the kingdom of God there is forgiveness, but it forgets about holy living. Real transformation in the image of Christ effectively drops out of the picture.

Paul addressed the first error in Rom. 6:1-2 and 1 Cor. 6:12-20. He condemns this way of thinking because it confuses dependence on grace with impotence in the face of sin. To summarize, let's say that the first error tries to protect justification by grace through faith. But it does so in a way that *subverts* sanctification—real transformation in Christ's image.

The **second** error is a mirror image of the first. This view stresses sanctification but effectively excludes the centrality of grace. It causes us to lose sight of our radical and continuing dependence on Christ's forgiveness. Rather than seeing discipleship as a journey in grace, we turn sanctification into strenuous performance-based perfectionism. In order to seem credible, such a view subtly depreciates the need for confession of sins, for grace, and for holiness.

This error drives us to shoulder a burden that should never be carried by a child of grace. If the first error expects too little from transformation, the second error claims too much. We've said that in the first error justification subverts sanctification. In the second error sanctification subverts justification. People who commit the second error mistake Christ's invitation to holy living as a call to perfectionism. Effectively, justification by grace through faith alone becomes a thing of the past.

> *In the kingdom of grace, the basis for our citizenship never changes.*

Christians must not forget that underlying all transformation rests a constant reliance upon a gracious and forgiving God. And although the first error gives too little attention to the commencement of sanctification, the second error gives too little attention to its continuation. Both errors miss the fact that Christian discipleship is an inaugurated and unending journey into God's transforming grace.

One error doesn't properly appreciate that the Kingdom is *already*. The second error forgets that the Kingdom is also *not yet*. The first error tends to collapse the *already* into the *not yet*. The other tends to collapse the *not yet* into the *already*.

These errors should not occur in Christ's Church. Neither arises from any fundamental inadequacy in the gospel of grace.

Indeed, each error mishandles the Good News, distorts its meaning, and scatters petals and leaves around muddy boots.

Grace, Faith, and Confession

In the kingdom of grace, the basis for our citizenship never changes. This is a glorious promise, a reason for rejoicing. It is also a strong warning against turning sanctification into a new works-righteousness. Sanctification is always the work of God's grace. Without end, God's forgiving, cleansing, and empowering presence forms the foundation for discipleship.

So what role does confession play in the holy life? Let's discuss it in a way that steers clear of the two errors we have just discussed.

In the Christian faith, confession has various shades of meaning. One sort of confession means affirming our faith in the triune God—the Father, His Son our Savior, and the Holy Spirit. We confess our faith, for example, when as a Body of believers we recite the Apostles' Creed or the Nicene Creed.[1] In another sense, we confess our faith in Christ by daily living as disciples. In this case, confession means living out what we affirm to be true about Jesus.

> *The confession of sin made by the children of God is driven by love and is an unmistakable expression of grace and faith.*

Another sort of confession means repenting for one's sins as a radical turning away from allegiance to the kingdom of darkness. This is the repentance associated with entering the kingdom of God and becoming a disciple of Christ. Confession of sin *also* applies to those who are already Jesus' disciples and who are being transformed by the Holy Spirit. One confession comes from a rebel, an estranged prodigal returning home. The other comes from a son or daughter of the Heavenly Father, a child of grace in need of forgiveness. A disciple's confession springs from a humble and honest recognition that he or she falls far short of the glory of God. The confession of sin made by the children of God is driven by love and is an unmistakable expression of grace and faith.

Disciples of Jesus should promptly and regularly ask forgiveness for imperfectly expressing, or failing to express, love for God and neighbor. Their confession comes because they love God. It does not dishonor Him. Instead, God is glorified when confession is moved by a grace-supported recognition that in many ways the Kingdom has not been manifested in us as it ought to be.

Although the Holy Spirit in sanctification establishes love for God and neighbor as the defining disposition of our lives, this does not mean that we perfectly express that love either to God or to our neighbor. All of us know that in many ways we do not. Learning to express love and to confess for failing to love are evidences that the Holy Spirit is establishing love as the defining disposition of our hearts. Love made perfect (as the norm for our lives), and loving perfectly, are two different things. The distinction must be kept clear. Confession for failing to show God's love as we ought to is love's work.

The Gift of Confession

Rightly understood, confession of sins by the disciples of Jesus is a gift of grace. Confession is both a privilege and a necessity (1 John 2:1-2).

The grace of God makes confession a *privilege* because it is God's gift not only to those who are alienated from Him but also to His children. It is a gift Christians should celebrate regularly. Confession is an important dimension of Christian freedom and transformation.

When we ignore our need for confession, we force ourselves into the unreasonable position of trying to be God. We're pretending, and we know it. Trying to be God is the most oppressive burden known to humanity. Those who shoulder the burden of perfectionism soon learn that it will either crush or harden them beyond recognition. Victims of this fruitless effort are not difficult to find. Some have even despaired of Christian discipleship. Others struggle endlessly to adjust to the burden. Once a person or a denomination falls victim to a view of Christian holiness shaped by "sinless perfectionism," they descend into self-deception. They succumb to an endless process of redefining and excusing various sins. In the interest of maintaining their perfectionism, they redefine sins of the spirit (for example, jealousy, greed, lust for power, divisiveness in Christ's Church, racism, sexism, and so on) as harmless human characteristics. Many struggling Christians who live under this bondage spend a lifetime trying to minimize or ignore sins that ought to be confessed and forgiven. Sadly, many persons in the interest of holy living choke off from their spirits the oxygen of honesty and the blood flow of God's grace.

The Holy Spirit wants to teach us that an important part of the Good News is that Christ releases us from the burden of perfection. He sets us free for life in the stream of responsible grace. The gospel of Christian freedom makes it unnecessary to claim for ourselves what belongs to God alone. We can depend solely on God's grace. This is good news! This is freedom!

People mistakenly shoulder the burden of perfection for many reasons. Some picture God as a tyrant who expects what no human being can deliver. Driven to perform, they never find a place to rest. Others may fall prey to the tyranny of perfectionism because their parents acted as though being finite was not good enough for humans. And some struggle with this error because their church presents sanctification as a graceless perfectionism. Such churches succeed only in helping people exchange one form of oppression for another.

. . . we wear masks, blame others, manufacture excuses, and live as deceptively as possible to cover sin.

Being free from the tyranny of perfectionism does not mean that grace sanctions irresponsibility. Life in the Spirit should be characterized by a diligent and responsible exercise of grace and Christian freedom. And part of our diligence is our responsibility to exercise the privilege of being honest about ourselves before God. This is more good news. After Adam sinned, dishonesty characterized his first encounter with God. When God tried to investigate what had happened, Adam blamed his predicament on Eve. From then on, hiding and blame-shifting became a defense mechanism used freely by individuals, families, and nations.

As a result, we wear masks, blame others, manufacture excuses, and live as deceptively as possible to cover sin. The greatest deception is our effort to convince God and ourselves that we are already good enough without Him. To be secure, we must reveal as little of the truth about ourselves as necessary. These attitudes are sin.

A perfectionist or oppressive notion of sanctification encourages the sin of dishonesty. It forces people to wear masks. It arises when grace ceases to be the real center of Christian discipleship.

William Greathouse urges us to keep the grace of God at the center of all we know about Christian discipleship. If we do, and if we live honestly before God and our neighbors, then, Greathouse says, we will not confuse Christian holiness with sinlessness. "Those filled with God's pure love," he says, "are still finite, human, and fallible. Inevitably, they fall short of God's perfect law of love and are guilty of 'involuntary transgressions.' The holiest of persons, therefore, need to pray, 'Forgive us our debts, as we forgive our debtors.'"[2]

The gift of confession makes it possible for Jesus' disciples to live honestly before God and others. Confession is a privilege of grace.

Confession as Responsibility

The grace of God makes confession a responsibility.

Several years ago, "Love means you never have to say you're sorry" was the theme of the popular book and movie titled *Love Story*. The slogan, which became very popular, revealed just how superficial our understanding of love can be. The truth is that in friendship or marriage, and certainly in Christian discipleship, a love that doesn't need to say "I am sorry" will soon be a love on the rocks. God's grace makes confession to God and neighbor necessary. The security that grace offers makes confession possible.

Disciples of Jesus who live honestly and sensitively in their churches, homes, and places of employment cherish the privilege and accept the responsibility of confession. As they honestly examine their extended participation in the church, their homes, and the world, they have no doubt about their inadequacies. They would be disappointed in a "holiness" that denies them the grace of confession.

The need to confess applies to instances in which we know we have failed to love God and neighbor as ourselves. It also applies to instances in which we fail and don't know it. Sometimes we offend others when we don't intend to. We might not even be aware that we have done so. Honest Christians have no interest in ignoring or denying this. The apostle Paul told the Corinthian Christians he thought he had been a good steward of the mysteries of God. So far as he knew, this was true. But he did not trust his knowledge as the basis for his reconciliation with God. Nor did he make the mistake of saying, "If I don't know of any offenses, then I don't have any reason for confession." Instead, Paul told the Corinthians, "It is a very small thing that I should be judged by you or by any human court. I do not even judge myself. I am not aware of anything against myself, but I am not thereby acquitted. It is the Lord who judges me" (1 Cor. 4:3-4, NRSV). For Paul, the grace of God made it unnecessary to excuse any offense— even ones unknown to him.

The Lord's Prayer is a petition based on grace.

The freedom and responsibility to confess *all* offenses is why Jesus taught His disciples to pray, "Forgive us our trespasses, as we forgive those who trespass against us." The Lord's Prayer is a petition based on grace. It was authored by the Lord of grace. The prayer meets human life head on. Some people have supposed that the Lord's Prayer was meant for sinners and not for saints. Wrong. The prayer is a prayer for the Church, for all of Jesus' disciples. No one graduates *into* holiness and *out of* the Lord's Prayer. The same Lord who taught His disciples to confess also called them to holy living.

Confession as Witness

Confession of sins by Christ's disciples is an important aspect of the Church's private and public witness to grace and holiness. For some Christians concerned about the public image of the Church, Christian holiness and confession of sin don't belong in the same sentence. Wrong again. In many instances, confession of sin by the Church and its members bears clear and convincing witness to the gospel of grace and to Christian holiness. By confessing our sins, we

Christians show our children, for example, that the grace of God is indeed the living center of our faith. When we don't confess our sins, we announce to those around us that the grace of God isn't really as important as we had earlier advertised. We communicate that the life of a Pharisee is the best life of all.

Theologian Dietrich Bonhoeffer addressed a prophetic word to the German state church at a time when it was in league with Adolf Hitler. Bonhoeffer said that only when the Church confesses its sins can it teach the world how to confess.

So what *is* there to confess? For starters, neither the Church as an institution nor we as individuals have spoken out against sin and injustice in society as we should have. We have not often enough raised our voices against child or spouse abuse and against improper care for the elderly. We have not sufficiently committed our resources against gambling and pornography. We have not set aside our own comforts and security to be committed intercessors for a broken world. We have not acted as advocates for the homeless and persons with mental illness who occupy our streets and sleep under our bridges. Many times the world has suffered because of the Church's absence.

A confessing Church witnesses to the excellence of a gracious God.

Jesus identified with sinners, and He calls us to do the same. There we will bear witness to the gospel by making all the confessions of grace. The Holy Spirit uses all dimensions of confession, including our confession of sins, to draw people to Christ. And if we are willing to receive the judgment directed against our failures, then we can receive the forgiveness and transformation that comes from God's grace. A confessing Church witnesses to the excellence of a gracious God.

Two beautiful and notable public expressions of what we are describing occurred in 1995. The first one took place in Atlanta in June. During its annual convention, the Southern Baptist Convention (SBC) asked "forgiveness from our African-American brothers and sisters." The SBC adopted a resolution on racial reconciliation that asked African-Americans for forgiveness for the role slavery played in the founding of the SBC. They made public confession for their past support of racism.

What prompted the Southern Baptists to make such a public confession? Were they no longer Christians? Did they no longer love God? Is that why they repented? No! Love for Christ and for their neighbors spurred their public confession. By adopting the resolution, Southern Baptists affirmed their faith in God's redeeming grace. They bore witness to the gospel and to their love for God and their neighbors. They were doing what should occur naturally for those who live in grace.

Was such a public confession dangerous? Might some observers have thought less of Southern Baptist discipleship? Might their witness have suffered? Let William Sheals, pastor of the Hopewell Baptist Church in Norcross, Georgia, a man who happens to be African-American, answer: "What a brave and awesome act of brotherhood and love!"

Two months later a second example of the church proclaiming the gospel by making public confession occurred half a world away, in Seoul. On August 14, 1995, five official delegates from the Japanese Church of the Nazarene visited Seoul. The delegation came bringing to the South Korean church a public confession for the atrocities the Japanese inflicted on the Koreans more than 50 years previously.[3] The written statement from the Japanese Nazarenes carried this title, "Confession of Responsibility of the Church of the Nazarene in Japan During the Second World War." The declaration of confession reads in part, "We . . . are sorry for the fact that we did not express our repentance officially for 48 years after the war, and we seek forgiveness for this also."

Rev. Yoshiaki Aoki, district superintendent of the Japan District, read the statement of confession to a gathering of more than 1,000 Korean Nazarenes. Afterward, Dr. Young-baik Kim of the Korean church embraced Rev. Aoki in an expression of forgiveness.

As Christians we have one responsibility that reigns above all others: we must worship the God of grace. We do so by confessing the meaning and power of His gift of grace in all its dimensions.

The Spirit has finished His work in none of us. Like the apostle Paul, we press on toward the goal for the prize of the upward call of God in Christ Jesus. And the God of all grace will lead the way (Phil. 3:12-16).

> *When you pray, say:*
> *Father, hallowed be your name.*
> *Your kingdom come.*
> *Give us each day our daily bread.*
> *And forgive us our sins, for we ourselves forgive*
>   *everyone indebted to us.*
> *And do not bring us to the time of trial*
>   (Luke 11:2-4, NRSV).

[For John Wesley] new birth is a social event that brings divine love down into the human family to take effect here. The nature of Christ's love is that it turns us immediately and inevitably toward others. Love that is self-contained, or purely and simply between the soul and God, is not "evangelical" love as Wesley understands it. It is not the intent of the love "which is shed abroad in our hearts" to draw human love to itself in the heavenly spheres, but to spend itself in the world in outpoured service. It is, as it were, poured through *our hearts into the world.*

—Theodore Runyon
Sanctification and Liberation

Christian ethics proceeds from the fact of justification as accomplished and given. . . . The ethical act, then, is simply an expression of the prior fact of justification; as it were, "subsequent" demonstration of the given justification.

—Helmut Thielicke
Theological Ethics

The primary social task of the Church is to be itself— that is, a people who have been formed by a story that provides them with the skills for negotiating the danger of this existence, trusting in God's promise of redemption. . . . Christians must serve the world on their own terms; otherwise the world would have no means to know itself as the world.

—Stanley Hauerwas
A Community of Character

CHAPTER *10*

Ethics and Agronomy

A FEW YEARS AGO ON AN ISLAND IN THE SOUTH PACIFIC, a man seriously offended the chiefs of his village. They banished him from the village and from his property. But the man took his case to civil court and won. The court ruled that the council of chiefs lacked the authority to deprive the man of his property. The court ordered them to allow the man to return.

But when the outcast returned, the chiefs met him at the edge of the village. The chiefs—among whom were some Christian ministers—told the man, "The courts may run the country, but we run this village. If you insist on returning, we will burn you alive." In spite of the threat, the man wanted to return. The chiefs had already filled a cooking pit with hot, glowing rocks. As the man entered the village, the chiefs advanced on him and herded him toward the pit, intending to push him in.

At that moment, two Evangelical pastors stepped between the islander and the glowing fire. The pastors told the chiefs that although what they were about to do would conform with ancient custom, it would not conform with the gospel of Jesus Christ the chiefs had embraced. The ancient ways, the two pastors said, must submit to new values born of the gospel.

Presently the chiefs backed away. The man's life was spared because the two courageous pastors understood the gospel of Christ. They risked their lives to teach others that out of the new way of *being* the gospel accomplishes, there must now proceed a new way of *doing*.[1]

Sixteenth-century reformer Martin Luther, in explaining the

relationship between salvation by grace alone and Christian ethics, said, "Good works do not a good man make, but a good man does good works." Much later John Wesley said that Christian ethics is the faith that works through love. Both men believed salvation is by grace through faith alone. But for each of these Protestant leaders, living a holy life by grace alone is inseparable from practicing the ethic born of the gospel. The grace of holiness unfailingly expresses itself, or replicates itself (to use the language of genetics), in an ethic

Practicing the Christian ethic is an essential part of holy living.

that has the gospel stamped all over it. In this chapter we want to explore the inseparable relationship between holy living and Christian ethics.

Jesus and Grapes

Jesus lived among people who were close to the earth. Agriculture was a prominent theme in His parables (Luke 8:4-15; 12:16-21; 13:18-19; 20:9-16). He often used vines and grapes, seeds and wheat, and trees and their fruit (Matt. 3:10; 7:16-20; Luke 6:43-44) to illustrate truths of the Kingdom. Vines should produce grapes that express the character of the vine (John 15:1-11). The vine and its grapes can be distinguished, but they can't be understood separately. Likewise, a farmer must know that if he plants wheat, he will harvest wheat. Human life in general is dependent on a regular and consistent reproduction of vines, seeds, and trees.

In the same way, for Jesus and the New Testament the kingdom of God is incomplete apart from the ethic it generates. One cannot exist apart from the other. The Christian ethic expresses the gospel of Jesus Christ. If the kingdom of God is a kingdom of grace, so is its ethic. The Kingdom's new order expresses itself in a distinctive way of life in the world. The ethic proclaims the Kingdom and witnesses to its authenticity. The Christian ethic is like an ambassador who embodies and speaks for the government he or she represents. Practicing the Christian ethic is an essential part of holy living.

The Christian Ethic and the Gospel of Grace

What is meant by the "Christian ethic"? The Christian ethic, or the ethic of the Kingdom, refers to the framework of principles through which the kingdom of God is concretely expressed. The Christian ethic shapes the moral practice of the citizens of the kingdom of God. Ethicists make a distinction between *ethics* and *morality*. *Ethics* is the framework of principles that undergird morality. *Morality* is the practice of ethics. Just as a farmer practices the science of agronomy in his or her farming, Christians practice the "science" of ethics in their morality. In popular usage, most of us don't maintain a formal distinction between ethics and morality. But properly, the terms are not interchangeable. Christians practice their morality according to the foundational principles of their ethic. But as any farmer could tell us, the practice of raising crops also impacts the principles of agronomy. Principles are sharpened by practice.

This chapter concentrates on the *nature* of the Christian ethic and not so much on the *practice* of Christian morality. It looks at the relationship between the Christian ethic and the gospel of grace. Our intention is to provide a broad framework for the practice of Christian morality.

When Jesus presented the ethic of the Kingdom, He always joined it to the grace of God (Matt. 18:23-35). According to Him, the Christian ethic is one important way of announcing that the kingdom of grace has come.

The Christian Ethic as Proclamation

The ethic of the Kingdom proclaims the God of the gospel and the good news of grace. It declares in moral practice the new way of being that the gospel creates. We say that the Christian ethic is a *new way of doing* that proceeds from, expresses, *a new way of being*. It reflects transformation by God's grace. The ethic expresses the kingdom of grace, and in so doing it becomes an agent of the Kingdom's growth and completion. All citizens of the Kingdom are to engage in this kind of proclamation.

The Christian ethic is a manifestation of the kingdom of grace. Sadly, some Christians don't understand this, which often leads them to compartmentalize their faith. It's an easy trap to fall into.

On the one hand, we're saved. On the other hand, we have a list of things we must do—as though they are not related to salvation. This is legalism. You see, the Christian ethic is *not* primarily about works—it's about grace. It's not about what we *can't* do, but what we *can* do, namely love God and our neighbor as ourselves. It is an ethic in which the Good News is expressed.

All legalistic efforts to separate the Kingdom from its ethic will finally collapse. Always Jesus has the last word: "I am the true vine. . . . Abide in me, and I in you. As the branch cannot bear fruit by itself, unless it abides in the vine, neither can you, unless you abide in me. . . . He who abides in me, and I in him, he it is that bears much fruit, for apart from me you can do nothing. If a man does not abide in me, he is cast forth as a branch and withers. . . . If you abide in me, and my words abide in you, ask whatever you will, and it shall be done for you" (John 15:1, 4-7, RSV).

As in all other aspects of the Kingdom, we must distinguish between the already and the not yet.

The kingdom of God is a realm of divine order and purpose. It is active, not static. The citizens of the Kingdom are the agents through which the Kingdom is realized. Only foolish persons attempt to become citizens without becoming agents of the Kingdom's ethic.

As in all other aspects of the Kingdom, we must distinguish between the *already* and the *not yet*. The Kingdom has been inaugurated. It's here. The contours of its completion are already discernible. When a spouse forgives and reconciles with an unfaithful husband or wife, we can see what the Kingdom looks like. But the Kingdom has not been consummated. Not everything toward which it moves is now possible. The same is true of the Kingdom's ethic. While much of what the Kingdom's ethic calls for is already possible, more of it is still taking shape, and some aspects of it won't be fulfilled until its consummation. For example, when the Kingdom comes in its fullness, the need to build prisons will no longer exist. But that's part of the *not yet*. Until then, our moral responsibility to protect children against sex offenders will likely make court systems and prisons necessary.

As Christians, we live between the *already* and the *not yet*. Understanding the creative tension between these two will save us from moral laziness on the one hand and naive optimism on the other. The New Testament teaches that even now the kingdom of light is forcing back the kingdom of darkness. The future of the kingdom of darkness has already been sealed. In practicing the ethic of the Kingdom, Christians rejoice over the *already*. They also press toward the *not yet*. Like a woman in labor, Paul said, Christians groan in anticipation of the Kingdom's completion (Rom. 8:18-25).

Characteristics of the Christian Ethic

With these understandings in place, let's now examine four characteristics of the Christian ethic.

First, the ethic of the Kingdom is an ethic of worship. It is God-centered. The ultimate purpose of the Christian ethic is to make God known and to glorify Him. This must be the focus of the Christian ethic, just as it is the focus of justification and sanctification.

Let us make an important distinction. As Christians, we stand in a religious, not a moral, relationship to God. We express worship to God, and we exercise moral responsibility toward our neighbor. Practicing the Christian ethic is a mode of worship. It is faith working through love for God and humanity. As strange as it might seem, persons are not the *primary* focus of Christian ethics. God is. We practice the Christian ethic before God and for His glory. Peter said that the purpose of all Christian discipleship, including Christian ethics, is that "God may be glorified through Jesus Christ" (1 Pet. 4:11, RSV).

Unless this first characteristic is kept firmly in place, Christian ethics will degenerate into all sorts of sub-Christian forms. When distorted, Christian ethics can become just one moral influence among others working for social improvement. When the primary goal of Christian ethics—to glorify God—is lost, then the significance of the cross and resurrection of Jesus evaporates in an atmosphere of general human goodwill.

The Christian ethic is rooted in the first commandment.

The Christian ethic is rooted in the first commandment, "You shall have no other gods before me" (Exod. 20:3). When asked about the greatest of the commandments, Jesus responded, "You shall love the Lord your God with all your heart, and with all your soul, and with all your mind. . . . And a second is like it, You shall love your neighbor as yourself" (Matt. 22:37, 39, RSV). As we have noted before, the primary dimension of discipleship is worship. This is also true of Christian ethics. The secondary dimension of discipleship is service to humanity and the rest of God's creation. But worship of God is the center that gives meaning and direction to service.

> *Good is not some independent moral standard to which God and man must conform.*

In numerous instances there are points of similarity between Christian ethics and philosophical or secular ethics. For example, both Christian ethics and secular ethics attempt to overcome racism. Sometimes people look at the points of similarity between Christian ethics and other types of ethics and conclude that there are no essential differences. They think that the religious language associated with Christian ethics is so much unnecessary lace and frill. Not so. An ethic that has worship of God as its defining center, as Christian ethics does, is substantially different from an ethic not grounded in worship.

If the primary orientation of the Christian ethic is worship, then *good*, as Christian ethics know it, will be *what God wills* in accordance with His own character and purposes. *Good* is not some independent moral standard to which God and man must conform. *Good* is good because God wills it—He does not will it because it is good. The Bible knows nothing of an independent *good* that transcends God. We may recall Jesus' words to the rich young ruler: "No one is good but God alone" (Luke 18:19, RSV).

When we do God's will, we do what is good. And in the Christian faith, good is always tested against what we know of God as revealed in Jesus Christ. All other notions of good—including those in the Old Testament—must submit to correction by what the life, death, and resurrection of Christ teach us. This means that a God-centered ethic is also a Christ-centered ethic. In Christ, the good is revealed and declared.

Second, the Christian ethic is an ethic of the gospel of the Kingdom. It announces the kingdom of God. The Christian ethic establishes what the gospel intends for all persons everywhere. The two are inseparable.

Put another way, practice of the Christian ethic is practice of the gospel. We don't receive the gospel and then decide whether or not we want to add the Christian ethic. The salvation of God can neither be understood nor received apart from the mode of life the gospel generates. The ethic proclaims the gospel in the way a beacon proclaims a New England lighthouse.

The Christian ethic begins with grace.

The Christian ethic begins with grace. It proceeds by grace. And its goal is the proclamation of the God of grace. Practicing the Christian ethic is a matter of being conformed by the Spirit to the image of Christ. Practice of the Christian ethic announces that in Jesus Christ a new order has come, and failure to do so denies that the Kingdom has come. By practicing the Christian ethic, Jesus' disciples declare the kingdom of God in concrete form.

The New Testament makes clear the inseparable relationship between the new birth in the Spirit and the practice of the Christian ethic. Paul said that "we are what he has made us, created in Christ Jesus for good works, which God prepared beforehand to be our way of life" (Eph. 2:10, NRSV).

A good way to illustrate the relationship between redemption and the Christian ethic is to examine the New Testament use of the indicative and imperative moods. In grammar, *mood* is the speaker's attitude toward the action a verb expresses. The *indicative* mood makes an assertion about what is regarded as fact. We use this mood on a regular basis. We may say, "I love you!" or "I sure do love chocolate ice cream!" A mother uses the indicative mood when she says to a child, "I told you yesterday to clean up this messy room!" Each of these involves a statement of fact.

The *imperative* mood, on the other hand, issues a command, wish, or exhortation. When a parent says to a teenage son, "Mow that lawn before you do anything else today!" the parent is using the imperative mood. It's an order.

The Christian ethic rests solidly upon a correct relationship between the indicative and the imperative. For Christian ethics, the two are inseparable, and the order cannot be reversed. First, on the basis of Christ's atoning work, we who have believed in Christ "have peace with God" (Rom. 5:1). This is true because God has made it so by His grace alone. By the Holy Spirit, God has united us with Christ in His death and has raised us to new life through His resurrection (6:1-11). God has declared His love for us and has freely reconciled us to himself. He leads us by His Spirit and declares us to be His children (8:15-17). These statements illustrate the indicative mood. They declare the fact of what God has done for us through Christ by grace. Paul's words to the Corinthians beautifully illustrate this: "You were washed, you were sanctified, you were justified in the name of the Lord Jesus Christ and by the Spirit of our God" (1 Cor. 6:11).

But the story isn't complete. The imperative—the command—is immediately and inseparably joined to the gospel's indicative. The indicative appears first, but the imperative always travels with it. Following immediately upon Paul's statement regarding our being crucified and raised with Christ comes the imperative: "Let not sin therefore reign in your mortal bodies. . . . Do not yield your members to sin as instruments of wickedness, but yield yourselves to God" (Rom. 6:12-13, RSV). The same thing occurs in Galatians: "Do not use your freedom as an opportunity for the flesh, but through love be servants of one another. . . . Walk by the Spirit and do not gratify the desires of the flesh" (Gal. 5:13, 16, RSV). Those who live by the Spirit's gift of redemption *must* then walk by the Spirit. Gift and command—indicative and imperative—are inseparable.

> *He never would have gained forgiveness by working off the debt.*

One of the most powerful portrayals of the close relationship between the indicative and the imperative occurs in Jesus' story of the unforgiving servant (Matt. 18:23-35). The servant's master freely forgave him of a debt equivalent to 150,000 years' wages. Jesus wants us to see that the servant's situation was hopeless. He never would have gained forgiveness by working off the debt. After being forgiven, the servant headed for home. On his way he encountered a fellow servant who owed him 100 days' wages. The first servant now had an opportunity to reexpress in moral practice the forgiveness the master had earlier extended to him.

Instead, he treated his fellow servant as though the master's forgiveness had not occurred. He demanded of his neighbor what had not been demanded of him. The servant was greatly interested in the indicative (gospel) for himself but had no interest in extending it to another. He refused to put the master's gift to work in an ethic.

Offering the indicative of regeneration and sanctification without requiring the imperative of the Christian ethic is what Dietrich Bonhoeffer called "cheap grace." On the other hand, demanding the imperative apart from the indicative produces legalism every time. Sometimes those who stress the importance of holy living forget that justification and sanctification are by grace through faith alone. Then the emphasis on holy living becomes a new moral tyranny. Only a "costly grace" that faithfully joins the indicative and the imperative can accurately express the gospel.

We are in Christ by grace alone, and we walk the Christian walk by the power of the Holy Spirit. By the Spirit's indwelling presence and power, we live the ethic of the gospel. When we live out the Christian ethic through the Spirit, Christ takes form in us and expresses who He is. As a result, the Christian also expresses who he or she is—a person transformed by God's grace. Christ in us—our hope of glory (Col. 1:27).

To summarize, let's say the Christian ethic arises from and expresses the gospel of Jesus Christ. It is the new way of doing that proceeds from a new way of being. The *being*—the gift of justification by grace through faith—is absolutely foundational to the *doing*—the faith that works through love. The ethical act is an expression of the prior fact of justification. Practicing the ethic is really a way of expressing the gift of redemption.

Third, the Christian ethic requires a life of responsible freedom. In the Christian ethic, freedom and responsibility are joined as fulfilling the grace of God. Neither can be understood apart from the other. Together each one achieves its highest possible expression. Throughout history the Church has struggled against attempts to divorce the two. Freedom apart from responsibility leads to moral license. Responsibility apart from Christian freedom leads to legalism.

Christian freedom means we are free from the law of sin and death. It also means we are free from a wrong relationship to the Law. But that's not all. Christian freedom means we are free *for* God, one's neighbor, and one's self. Jesus linked freedom with responsibility when He told His disciples, "If you keep my commandments, you will abide in my love" (John 15:10, RSV). He also told them, "By this my Father is glorified, that you bear much fruit, and so prove to be my disciples" (v. 8, RSV). The apostle Paul echoed the words of Jesus when he told the Galatians, "For you were called to freedom, brothers and sisters; only do not use your freedom as an opportunity for self-indulgence, but through love become slaves to one another" (Gal. 5:13, NRSV).

One of the marks of responsible freedom is that it demonstrates religious, moral, and cultural creativity.

The Corinthian Christians had a difficult time joining freedom and responsibility. Some delighted in freedom but wanted nothing to do with responsibility. Others were so consumed by responsibility that it degenerated into legalism, and freedom was lost. The Book of Jude was written in part to rebuke those in the Church who were living irresponsibly. The writer describes them as "ungodly persons who pervert the grace of our God into licentiousness and deny our only Master and Lord, Jesus Christ." (v. 4, RSV). Such persons are "wild waves of the sea, casting up the foam of

their own shame" (v. 13, RSV). The gospel is simple, and it is extended to all persons. But learning to join Christian freedom to
Christian responsibility in the Church, the home, and the world
will require patience and discipline.

The true fruit of Christian freedom is the fruit of the Spirit
(Gal. 5:16-26). Any exercise of freedom that shows disregard for the
well-being of the Body of Christ introduces anarchy and reinstates
slavery (Rom. 14:1-23; 1 Cor. 6:12-20; 9:1-23). The kingdom of
grace, Paul told the Roman Christians, consists neither of an irre-
sponsible disregard for the well-being of one's neighbor nor of
blind obedience to rules and decrees. Instead, "the kingdom of
God is . . . righteousness and peace and joy in the Holy Spirit. The
one who thus serves Christ is acceptable to God and has human
approval" (14:17-18, NRSV).

One of the marks of responsible freedom is that it demonstrates religious, moral, and cultural creativity. The Christian ethic
presents to us possibilities for community, for expanding the
meaning of neighbor, and for personal growth that have never appeared before. Through the Spirit, for example, we discover that
the old destructive ways of viewing others have been set aside by
Christ. Paul Ricoeur says that through the exercise of responsible
freedom, the Holy Spirit "goads" the moral limitations and satis-
factions to which we have grown accustomed.

Growing in responsible freedom doesn't mean we disregard
moral norms. But it does mean we learn how to act redemptively
when the best conceivable outcome is no longer an option. That, by
the way, was how the gospel reached us. The best conceivable option would have been that Adam and Eve had never sinned. But
their sin did not stop God from acting creatively and redemptively.
The ethic of the Kingdom calls us to do the same—practice the
grace of God. This is how the Good News reached the Samaritan
woman at the well (John 4:4-42). The best conceivable options—
one husband, two kids, nice home—had passed her by. But the
gospel of Jesus Christ did not. As we grow in responsible freedom,
we fine-tune our alertness to ways in which more and more of life
can be claimed for the kingdom of grace.

Responsible freedom will always seek to act with the future in
mind. The apostle Paul sent Onesimus the slave back to Philemon,

his owner, because according to Roman law, he could have done nothing else. But even then, he instructed Philemon to receive Onesimus "no longer as a slave, but . . . as a dear brother" (v. 16). With his sensitivity to the social and moral creativity of the gospel, Paul introduced a principle and spirit that would eventually spell the end of slavery in Christian lands.

Fourth, the Christian ethic is a form of storytelling. Christian faith and life are shaped within a community that exists because it has heard and received the great story of God's freeing and sustaining love. The Church both transmits and is part of the story. We first hear and learn to practice the story in the Church. We then tell the story and practice the ethic in the world. Over and over, we in the Church must ask, "What kind of community ought we to be if we are to be faithful to the convictions that form the Christian story?"

The story that shapes the Church and its members is all about the Creator-Redeemer God. It recounts God's relationship with a people He has called into existence. In turn, they pass along the story of God joyfully and correctly. To become a good storyteller is one goal of Christian discipleship. We place ourselves in the hands of the master Storyteller. When we do, the Lord brings our story into conformity with His story. The master story forms in us the image of Christ.

Merely hearing the story without being transformed by it would be pointless. Jesus ended some of His stories by saying, "Go and do likewise." The central convictions that form the story ought to shape and fill in all the contours of our lives. This is holy living. It is "story" living.

In his book *The Body,* Chuck Colson tells a story that beautifully illustrates all we have discussed in this chapter. Rusty Woomer was a convicted murderer awaiting execution in the South Carolina State Prison in Columbia. The story of Rusty's childhood and teen years was one of domestic turmoil and abuse by a drunken father. He lived in fear, hunger, and poverty. While still a very young man, Rusty participated in a crime spree in South Carolina that left four persons murdered and two seriously wounded. In prison, the demons of despair had almost succeeded in reducing him to an animal. His long, dirty, blond hair and beard were matted and greasy. Cockroaches crawled all over him and his cell.

One evening Bob McAllister, director of communications and deputy chief of staff to Governor Carroll Campbell, found Rusty. Bob regularly engaged in ministry to prisoners on death row. On his way out of the prison that evening, Bob stopped in front of Rusty's cell, noting his horrifying condition. In the name of Jesus Christ, Bob McAllister rebuked the demons of sin and despair. He called upon Rusty to "just say the name 'Jesus.' Call on Jesus." Christ heard Rusty's mumbled prayer and came into his life. The transformation was startling. Rusty's growth in Christ was remarkable.

Bob petitioned Governor Campbell to commute Rusty's death sentence to life imprisonment. The governor wrestled with the request and with Rusty's remarkable story. But he concluded that he could not "intervene in the workings of the judicial process"— Rusty Woomer would be executed as the court had ordered.

On the evening before Rusty's scheduled execution, he received into his cell an unexpected visitor: South Carolina's top prison official, Corrections Commissioner Parker Evatt. Parker is a committed Christian who is firmly opposed to capital punishment, but his job required him to uphold and enforce the laws of the state. In the cell that night were Rusty, Parker, Bob, and four others. Together the men prayed for God's strength and for God's peace upon each other. They celebrated the Lord's Supper.

As had happened many times before, the Church, the Body of Christ, had gathered in a prison cell to hear and tell the story of Jesus. The laws of the state, duly instituted by the people, were about to be enforced—Rusty would die. But the somber setting in which the Church had gathered on the eve of Rusty's scheduled execution could not prohibit the presence and creativity of the resurrected Christ. He came and displaced the gloom of death just as He had done on the first Easter morning.

Parker Evatt was bound by oath of office to carry out his responsibilities. But as a teller of *the* story, he was unwilling to settle for those limits. He had to find a way to embody the story. And so he descended into the gloom of death row to bear witness to

Christ. Through the Spirit, Parker Evatt creatively expressed the grace of God. In that prison cell the whole story of the gospel came alive. No civil law demanded that Parker Evatt be in that cell. But the gospel, which has seen the inside of many jails, placed Parker there. And by being there, he announced the coming of the kingdom of grace. As he celebrated the Lord's Supper with Rusty, Parker and the others voiced their confidence that the kingdom of God would be fulfilled.[2]

Now to him who is able to keep you from falling and to present you without blemish before the presence of his glory with rejoicing, to the only God, our Savior through Jesus Christ our Lord, be glory, majesty, dominion, and authority, before all time and now and for ever. Amen (Jude 24-25, RSV).

[For John Wesley] sanctification—or Christian perfection—is not in the final analysis to be defined negatively, as the absence of sin, but positively, as the active presence of love expressed not only in word but in deed: from God to humanity, from humanity to God; from God through human beings, to their fellow human beings. This is the power of the Kingdom that begins to exercise its humanizing impact in the present age.

—Theodore Runyon
Sanctification and Liberation

God's gift of freedom makes persons free to be not more and not less than human.

—Karl Barth
The Humanity of God

The doctrine of the image of God is comprehensible in its deepest meaning only from the center of divine self-revelation. Behind the Christian doctrine of man stands, as its basic foundation, the faith in that Man [Christ] in whom both the mystery of God and the secret of man have been revealed in one; the belief that the creator of the universe attaches Himself to humanity; that He, in whose creative word the whole structure of the Universe has its foundation, has made known as His world purpose the restoration and perfection of His image in humanity; that therefore not only the history of humanity, but the history of the whole Cosmos shall be consummated in God-humanity.

—Emil Brunner
Christianity and Civilization

CHAPTER 11

To Canterbury They Go

THE CANTERBURY TALES IS ONE OF THE BEST-KNOWN works in the English language. Late in the 14th century, Geoffrey Chaucer spun these famous tales about 30 or so pilgrims traveling to Canterbury to visit the shrine of Archbishop Thomas à Becket, who was martyred in 1170.

The pilgrims represented a cross section of medieval society. They included people who were related principally to the land (a knight and a squire), some who were related principally to the church (a monk and a nun), and others who were related principally to the professions (a lawyer and a doctor). The pilgrims agreed that on the way to Canterbury, each one would tell two stories. On the return journey they would do the same. Chaucer's genius made each person come alive through his or her tale.

Although the pilgrims came from different places, and although each one had a different history, all were united in a single journey, a shared story, and a common purpose and destination. And so the great tale begins:

> When April with its sweet showers pierce the root of
>   March's drought . . .
> Especially from the ends of every county
> Of England to Canterbury they go.

Jesus the Storyteller

In its own way, the New Testament relates a tale of pilgrims, each with his or her own story to tell. Fishermen, tax collectors, prostitutes, Pharisees, demoniacs, and a few who had been raised from the dead. Think of what Chaucer could have done with *this* bunch!

These New Testament characters are on a journey, not to the shrine of a martyr, but to formation in the image of Christ. They are journeying *from* grace and *into* grace. They are journeying into personhood. Jesus is the Narrator and Guide.

Formation of persons in the image of Christ is one good way of describing the life of Christian holiness. It is the process by which Christ comprehensively takes form in us. An important dimension of the doctrine of creation, the gospel, and Christian worship is God's great regard for us as persons. Christ tells His story through us, but He does not treat us as though we are mindless puppets. Rather, He considers us His real dialogue partners in whom personhood at its highest levels is brought to pass.

Chaucer set out to write the stories of these pilgrims (he completed only a fifth of the stories he had planned). Jesus is creating stories for untold millions. Taken together, the lives of Christians reflect the wide spectrum of grace. The people who are the subjects of the many stories compose the *koinonia*, the Body of Christ.

Is It All Right to Be Human?

One of the central themes of the story of grace is that it is good to be human. This may seem to be an obvious statement, but throughout the history of the Christian faith, the Church has had to battle against one heresy after another that wanted to label humanity inherently and hopelessly evil. In one form or another, these movements have identified sin with physical, fleshly existence.

Unlike some of the Greeks and others, the Hebrews did not sharply divide the human person into earthly and spiritual spheres (soul, mind, spirit, and body). The Hebrews didn't have to.

We know that the whole earth is full of His glory.

They didn't have a disregard for the earthly. Instead, they believed that God created the world—everything—and called it good. They believed He created Adam and Eve in His image and called them very good. The Hebrews also believed that God could associate with, even inhabit, what He had created. Doing so would not jeopardize His holiness. Consequently, they could think of personhood in holistic, integrated terms. They could distinguish various dimensions of a person, but they found it unnecessary to make rigid distinctions. What they believed about God as Creator directly affected what they believed about the goodness of human existence.

In many beautiful ways, Jesus celebrated the goodness of creation and the excellence of being human.

For the Hebrews, the goal of communion with God was not to abandon the world as incurably evil, as would later be true of the gnostics. It was instead to worship God through participation in the whole created order—everything He had made. God meant for Adam and Eve to be stewards through whom the creation would fulfill its divinely authored purposes. The whole creation participates in worshiping God by its very existence because it reflects God as Creator. We know that the whole earth is full of His glory. In fact, the psalmist calls on creation to praise God (Ps. 148). Creation can even serve as a means through which God communicates and gives himself to humanity. Hence the significance of the manger, the Cross, the bread, and the wine as instruments of God's self-disclosure.

We have said that according to the Bible, being human is good. God can be known by people who live in *this* world. He is praised *in* and *by* His creation. The Scriptures affirm this, and the New Testament's appraisal of earthly existence lays the foundation for the gracious construction of personhood.

The incarnation of God in Jesus of Nazareth should forever erase any lingering suspicions regarding God's relationship to creation. In many beautiful ways, Jesus celebrated the goodness of creation and the excellence of being human. He was born in a manger and reared in a carpenter's home. He surrounded himself with fishermen and tax collectors. According to John, Jesus' first public miracle occurred amidst festivities when people were celebrating marriage, family, and the everyday stuff of life.

When Jesus wanted to communicate most intensely what His life on earth meant, He did not call for assistance from angels and heavenly powers. Instead, on the evening of the Lord's Supper, He distributed bread and wine to His disciples. He said, "This is my body which is given for you. . . . This cup which is poured out for you is the new covenant in my blood" (Luke 22:19-20, RSV). According to John, on that same evening Jesus poured water into a common basin, tied a towel around His waist, and washed His disciples' feet (John 13:1-11).

The early Christian church succeeded in affirming the full humanity of Christ only after a difficult struggle against opponents of the Incarnation. There were persons in the Early Church who thought the humanity of Jesus was a scandalous error created by people ignorant of how evil fleshly existence is. Because they thought the physical world was hopelessly evil, they insisted that God could not become fully incarnate in a human life. Doing so would endanger His deity. So the opponents of the Incarnation developed numerous ways to explain how Christ could become Redeemer without becoming fully human. Usually they said that He only appeared to be human and only appeared to die on the Cross. Some said that Christ's humanity was an illusion used to trick Satan.

No excuses are made in telling the sorry story.

The authors of the New Testament would have none of it. They were firmly rooted in Hebraic faith and knew this world wasn't the result of cosmic error or fallen and evil deities. They also knew that one goal of redemption is the restoration of the *whole* creation, not just some marginal part of it. The gospel of hope they preached attracted people to the gospel then just as it does now.

The struggle against those who would subvert the incarnation of God in Jesus of Nazareth shows up clearly in the Gospel according to John. Against opponents of the Incarnation and the goodness of God's creation, John declared, "The Word became flesh and dwelt among us, full of grace and truth; we have beheld his glory, glory as of the only Son from the Father. . . . And from his fullness have we all received, grace upon grace" (John 1:14, 16, RSV). Anyone who wants to deny the full humanity of Jesus and the goodness of God's creation must first dismantle the Gospel of John.

The redemption that the Incarnate Christ accomplished in His death and resurrection is directed toward the whole created order. The apostle Paul knew that creation had somehow been negatively affected by sin, but he was confident that it, too, shared an inheritance in Christ's atonement. "The creation itself will be set free from its bondage to decay and [will] obtain the glorious liberty of the children of God," he wrote (Rom. 8:21, RSV).

Paul shared the Old Testament belief that God is the Creator. He rebuked those who wanted to depreciate God's creation as an unfit home for Christians. He firmly rejected the notion that to live according to the Holy Spirit, Christians must escape fleshly existence. He told the Christians in Rome that through the power of Christ's resurrection, they could now live *according to the Holy Spirit* in the flesh (which for Paul includes the whole created order). For Paul, alienation from God resides not *in the flesh* but in living *according to the flesh* (Rom. 8:1-8).

Let there be no mistake: Paul did not condemn creation as though it were the cause of life according to the flesh. He pointed the finger of blame directly at sin (Rom. 8:3-4). Both the Old and New Testaments candidly rehearse the damage sin has done to human existence, to creation, and to God's relationship with His world. No excuses are made in telling the sorry story. And yet, no matter how hard sin tries to divorce God from His creation, it fails. God raised up Jesus from the grave!

What does all this mean? A major part of its meaning is that *being human is good.* This is a message not founded on secularism or Hollywood hype. Instead, it rests upon the incarnation, cross, and resurrection of Jesus Christ. It is founded in the holiness and love of God the Creator, the goodness of His creation, and the person and work of Jesus Christ.

Journey into the New Humanity

We have seen that Christ is the Author of a new humanity. This humanity has both earthly dimensions and dimensions that transcend the earthly. The old humanity lives in service and bondage to the earthly (life after the flesh), and the end is death. It treats what God made as though it *were* God. But the new humanity is lived *in* the flesh, *by* the Spirit, *in worship of* God, and *in celebration of* God's creation. Anyone who wants to make less of God's grace, less of the Christian faith, and less of human life than this should learn to enjoy defeat. For the Word of God stands against him or her.

The call to discipleship is an invitation to human wholeness in the world, into a celebration of what it means to be fully human before the Creator God who rejoices in His creation. It is a journey into Christ that always grows richer and is never finished. The Spirit of grace is always constructing personhood in community.

No one is so wounded that he or she cannot participate in the Christian story.

Just as the Church struggles to protect the humanity of Jesus, it must also work to keep the sanctifying, humanizing work of the Holy Spirit firmly grounded in earthly existence. For some, God would look far more successful if He would tackle something a little less thorny than life. And so they seem to develop schemes of redemption for angels who don't have to rear children in single-parent families, wrestle with temptations, or serve as union stewards. They have lofty aspirations for those who don't have to care for elderly parents, make difficult decisions in voting booths, recover from broken marriages, or pick up the pieces after careers have collapsed at midlife. Whenever these builders of dream-worlds appear, a lowly Galilean who went to parties and rode a borrowed donkey into Jerusalem brings them back to earth.

In the Bible, worship of God includes the construction and fulfillment of personhood. Only as we worship God can we come to know what being human means. The journey into God's grace is indeed a liberating journey into personhood.

In one important sense, all of us begin the journey from the same point. We embark by confessing our sins and our radical dependence on God's grace. We begin by abandoning the old life and by becoming new creations in Christ Jesus (see 2 Cor. 5:17). But in another important sense, none of us starts at the same place. As we have seen, all of us come to the journey of grace with our own frames of reference. We each have a particular history that affects the way we progress along the way. We come from differing religious, domestic, emotional, moral, intellectual, and social backgrounds. The histories of some persons have been positive and productive; the histories of others have been negative and destructive. Christ asks no one to deny his or her history in order to encounter the fullness of His grace. No one is so wounded that he or she cannot participate in the Christian story. In recreating His story in us, Christ takes our stories seriously and redeems them so that they can no longer stand against us. Old things pass away, and all things become new (again, see 2 Cor. 5:17).

The gracious Christ demonstrates His love in the way He greets us and inaugurates the journey into personhood. He meets us where we are and gives himself to us right there. No one need despair because he or she doesn't have the history of someone else. When Jesus spoke, Mary Magdalene, Matthew the tax collector, and Zacchaeus each knew He was speaking to *him or her*.

God's grace will shape us as individuals. Some persons bring past failures and scars that will impact the way Christ takes form in them. Some persons bring deeply held prejudices that will have to be chiseled away by the Holy Spirit. Others have engaged in habits that have impaired their ability to make clear judgments and choices. Still others have experienced such destructive relationships that the ability to trust will have to be constructed from the ground up. Whether blessings or curses, we must bring everything there is of us to the journey of grace. The whole of us is subject to redemption (Rom. 12:1-2; 1 Thess. 5:22-23).

While Christ does set us free for God, for our neighbor, and for ourselves, His grace in our lives is far more important than the degree of freedom we may be able to achieve. The Spirit imposes no uniform rate of progress on the pilgrims. And though God expects all of us to exercise grace responsibly, the journey into grace doesn't finally grind down to oppressive performance. As the parable of the talents makes clear, not everything is expected of everyone (Luke 19:12-27). Many people have tragedies in their histories that might seriously restrict the level of growth they can achieve. No one should make the mistake of imposing a tyrannical level of achievement on any of God's children. Only He is their Lord, and He knows them far more intimately than anyone else.

Though histories do impact the way grace is formed in us, normally they don't immobilize us. If we've been fortunate to have a good history, that's no cause for arrogance. If our life has been less than ideal, that's no excuse for carelessness. No matter what our background, as disciples we submit ourselves to formation in Christ and to His formation in us. Discipleship means simply becoming an obedient, pliable student in the school of Jesus.

> *Discipleship means simply becoming an obedient, pliable student in the school of Jesus.*

The gracious formation of personhood does not occur accidentally. Many means of grace are available to us. Some are more pivotal than others. Receiving the proclamation of the Word and partaking of the sacraments of baptism and the Lord's Supper are foundational for a gracious construction of personhood. Other important means of grace include prayer, study of the Scriptures, and sharing the Spirit's gifts within the Body of Christ.

The Gracious Construction of Personhood

With all this in place, we can now identify *four* principles that should operate in the gracious construction of personhood. The principles touch our relationships with God, our neighbor, and ourselves. They affect the religious, moral, and cultural dimensions of the human spirit.

The first principle is increased awareness. Jesus told Nicodemus that the things of the Spirit are given to those who are born of the Spirit (John 3:6-12). When we were dead in trespasses and sins, the things of the Spirit did not even register with us. Our faculties for receiving the things of the Spirit were darkened. When we submit to the gracious construction of personhood, we must be prepared for a marvelous opening of our spiritual faculties. The old reality will pass away, and all things will become new. We will be renewed in the inner person. The conscience will be evangelized, *Christianized*, by the Holy Spirit. All relationships and values will be reexamined in light of the person of Jesus and the kingdom of God. Anyone who tries to drag along the old idols, hoping to establish them in Christ's kingdom, will be disappointed.

The principle of increasing awareness means that under the impact of the Spirit at least the following occurs:

+ We become sensitive to all that has stood against the new humanity in Christ, both in ourselves and in the world around us. Increasingly we become aware of the forces that struggle against the kingdom of God, and increasingly we become aware of how those powers have impacted our own values, attitudes, and so on. Awareness and honesty journey together. We come to know ourselves and our contexts more truly in the light of Christ.

+ We become more aware of the demonic—namely, any effort by any power to elevate itself to a position of deity or to alienate us from God, our neighbor, or ourselves. Any power that wants to occupy God's throne is demonic. The world is awash in such powers, some evident and some subtle, but all destructive. The apostle Paul said that "we are not contending against flesh and blood, but against the principalities, against the powers, against the world rulers of this present darkness, against the spiritual hosts of wickedness in the heavenly places" (Eph. 6:12, RSV).

+ We feel solidarity with those who suffer injustice. Solidarity includes speaking with and for them, remembering and recounting their stories.

+ We grow in the wisdom that comes from above (James 3:17-18). This wisdom cultivates discernment into the kingdom of evil, which, for instance, sets people against themselves, one race against another, or family member against family member. Christian wisdom seeks the peace of God. The Christian "wise person" is not someone who lives aloof from the conflict between the kingdom of God and the demonic. Instead, he or she learns the enemy's movements and knows how through intercessory prayer, for instance, to employ the whole armor of the Spirit.

✦ We get to know the creative power of the Holy Spirit. Paul told the Corinthian Christians, "Though we live in the world we are not carrying on a worldly war, for the weapons of our warfare are not worldly but have divine power to destroy strongholds" (2 Cor. 10:3, RSV). He admonished the Ephesian Christians to "take the whole armor of God, that you may be able to withstand in the evil day" (6:13, RSV). Peter, who was at one time very quick to trust his own resources, urged his readers to "grow in the grace and knowledge of our Lord and Savior Jesus Christ" (2 Pet. 3:18, RSV).

✦ We become aware of our God-given dignity as persons, without respect to gender, race, or nationality. We are the children of God, and we glorify Him by exercising the gifts and potential He has given us. These may include artistic abilities, professional interests, intellectual dispositions, and so on. God's children glorify Him by becoming as complete as His gifts and power provide. This is dignity.

Learning to practice responsible Christian freedom will likely take some getting used to.

The second principle is increasing freedom. This principle is especially prominent in Paul's description of life in the Spirit (Rom. 8:1-17). Because of what he knew about the grace of God, Paul told the Corinthian Christians, "All things are yours, whether Paul or Apollos or Cephas or the world or life or death or the present or the future, all are yours; and you are Christ's; and Christ is God's" (1 Cor. 3:21-23, RSV). There it is—Christian freedom. But the letters to the Corinthians reveal that those young Christians were just beginning the process of embodying the freedom Christ had already given to them.

Learning to practice responsible Christian freedom will likely take some getting used to. Paul was greatly alarmed over the Galatian Christians, because they were moving away from, not toward, Christian freedom. Likewise, the most critical factor for the Corinthians was the direction in which they were moving. American civil rights leader Martin Luther King Jr. held a Ph.D. from Boston University and had gained world recognition. But he said that when he confronted the fierce police dogs in Birmingham, Alabama, and the powerful racist structure that controlled them, he discovered that there was still too much bondage to racism left inside him.

Freedom is a gift that must be lived and practiced responsibly. All of our emotions, aspirations, fears, and urges should be brought under the practice of responsible freedom. Freedom is one of the arts of grace.

> *Legalism does not promote moral imagination; it sticks to the status quo.*

Growing accustomed to living as a free child of grace will happen as the Holy Spirit works in us. We will increasingly be set free from the Law as something that stands over us and will begin to sense the law of the Spirit being *written on the fleshly tablets of our hearts* (2 Cor. 3:3). The Law will rule us less and less. The way of the Lord will shine through us more and more.

Christian freedom should promote moral imagination in us. This means we will grow in our ability to think about what *could be*, rather than being satisfied with what *is*. Legalism does not promote moral imagination; it sticks to the status quo. But God seeks what might be, rather than settling for what is. Moral imagination lay behind the passage of child labor laws, the cessation of chattel slavery, the success of the women's suffrage movement, and legislation against spouse abuse. We now take all these changes in our society for granted. But these boundaries were broken by people of great moral imagination.

The third principle is increasing relatedness. In a sense, this balances the principle of increased freedom. The principle of relatedness means increasing sensitivity to others. It involves expanding the meaning of *neighbor* (Luke 10:29-37). Many of us, for instance, have been conditioned to deny full personhood to some people because of their gender, color, nationality, or so on. As we journey into grace, we must increasingly recognize and respect the dignity and value of others and dismantle the old prejudices. It is impossible to claim the riches of personhood for myself and then deny those riches to others. The gracious construction of personhood has been arrested in too many Christians because they have allowed the old stereotypes to continue deciding who persons are or who they are not (2 Cor. 5:16).

The principle of increasing relatedness is the principle of community. It teaches us how to answer the question, Who is my neighbor? It teaches us to answer the question, Am I my brother's keeper? Through the Holy Spirit's patient construction, the children of God see more clearly the implications of saying that all persons are created in the image of God.

The fourth principle is increased transcendence. This might sound like removal from the world. Instead, this principle involves learning to view more and more of life sacramentally, recognizing the sacred in the midst of the secular. It has nothing to do with escapism or New Age nonsense. It is simply fine-tuning our ability to see God at work in the day-to-day stuff of life. As we practice the spiritual disciplines, our discernment will increase. We will see the same tendency in the midst of our vocation, parenting, deeds of mercy, and in the use of leisure.

⎯⎯⎯

So what does the gracious construction of personhood have to do with Christian holiness? Everything. The story that Christ is telling in and through us is the story of himself. Christian formation of personhood is really Christ taking shape in us. Beautifully, in the life of Christian holiness, as Christ takes form in us, He cultivates an ever-expanding fulfillment of our humanity as well. Happily, growth in Christian holiness includes concretely exploring and fulfilling the meaning of *person*.

It is the Father's good pleasure to renew the face of the earth. Surely all these evil things shall come to an end, and the inhabitants of the earth shall learn righteousness . . . and all the kingdoms of the earth shall become the kingdoms of our God.

—John Wesley
The Works of John Wesley, 5:277

God not only desires to live in the heart but also in the world. He desires societal forms that provide the best possible channels for the forces of his holy love.

—Hendikus Berkhof
Christian Faith

In the word of God that raised Jesus from the grave, in the word which calls those who are guilty into righteousness, the meaning of history comes into the present and does not allow the present to remain as it is. The word of God makes the present the advancing front line which is freed from the past and is propelled into God's oncoming newness.

—Jurgen Moltmann
Hope and Planning

[For John Wesley] the process of sanctification is the purification of history, overcoming the elements of society and in the life of the individual that cannot stand at the latter day.

—Theodore Runyon
Sanctification and Liberation

CHAPTER *12*

Sanctifying the Secular

ONE OF THE MOST SPELLBINDING STORIES WRITTEN BY Robert Louis Stevenson is *Kidnapped*. It's about young David Balfour who, after the death of his parents, set out to seek his fortune. His thieving uncle, Ebenezer Balfour, who had hated David's father, desired David dead as well. Ebenezer wanted to make sure David would never receive his rightful inheritance, the House of Shaws.

To carry out his evil scheme, Ebenezer posed as David's friend and then sold him as a slave to a brutal ship's captain. Captain Hoseason and his officers were murderers and thieves. David was forced against his will to do Hoseason's bidding aboard the *Covenant of Dyart*.

The unfolding drama of David's struggle to escape the *Covenant of Dyart* and to gain his rightful inheritance has riveted the attention of children and adults for more than a century. Although Robert Louis Stevenson didn't intend for *Kidnapped* to be read as a Christian parable, it can easily be interpreted that way.

The World: Crew Member or Slave?

One of the most important questions a Christian engaged in the holy life must ask and answer is, What does God think of the world?[1]

On any given day, a British man-of-war might have sailed past the *Covenant of Dyart* on which David Balfour was a slave. The crew might have seen David working diligently for the murderous Hoseason. Imagine that you were a crew member of the man-of-war. As your ship sailed past the *Covenant*, your eyes happened to fix momentarily on David. As you watched him work, what conclusions might you have drawn about him? Appearances might have led you to conclude that because David was working so diligently, he was surely a willing and paid member of the crew—just another young man out to seek his fortune on the high seas. Your casual observations would not have told you the truth about David. In a few moments, your attention probably would have been drawn elsewhere. You assumed that your brief thoughts regarding the cabin boy were correct, when in fact you had missed your chance to help free a slave.

The creation seems to be a willing crew member in Satan's hire.

Through the centuries, many Christians have looked at the world and have drawn similar conclusions. They have observed the world as it does sin's bidding, and they have concluded that the world is in league with Satan himself. The creation seems to be a willing crew member in Satan's hire. Its metals are used to make implements of war. Its men and women pervert human sexuality to satisfy unbridled lust. Its barley and grapes can be made to intoxicate and dull the mind. Its kings and princes, presidents and senators, have used the levers of government to oppress the poor and betray public trust.

Based on appearances, many Christians have concluded that this world is just as evil as the captain on whose ship it often serves. Consequently, in contempt they have turned away from the world, abandoned it to eventual shipwreck, and written it off as hopelessly evil. They believe Christians have no lasting interest in the world and should regard it as God's enemy. The holy life must be lived in active rejection of the world.

Is this an accurate presentation of God's relationship to the world? Does He view the world as an incorrigible and destructive pirate who deserves the hangman's noose?

Or has the world been kidnapped? Is the creation really a child of God's grace, called into existence by the extravagance of God's love, an object of redemption even as we are? Perhaps the world's service to lust, violence, greed, and so forth, is an unwilling one. Maybe the world longs for liberation from a bondage it did not choose. Perhaps creation is rooted in God's love and redemption even as we are. Could it be that as Christians our attitude toward the world should be that of a rescuer, an advocate? Maybe the good news that God has acted redemptively in Christ is good reason for the heavens to rejoice and the earth to be glad (Ps. 96:10-13), for they, too, are included in redemption. Maybe God knows that what others see on the surface is not the world's true character—past, present, or future.

Perhaps God himself is the world's untiring Rescuer, diligently seeking to restore the creation to its rightful place before Him. What if it were to turn out that the world is a child of honorable birth and glorious inheritance?

If this second scenario were correct, what difference should it make in a Christian's relationship to the world? How would viewing the world as a child of grace affect the way we understand and live the holy life?

A Child of Grace

We know from Psalm 96 that the announcement that God reigns is heard as good news by all creation. But what about the New Testament? Does it help settle the question regarding how God assesses creation? Yes, it provides clear answers.

First, let's look at what Paul claims Christ's relationship to creation to be.

If creation and the social orders in which we live are willing allies of sin, then should we not expect to find our Lord putting as much distance as possible between himself and the world? If God is in the process of divesting himself of this creation, then the world should show only vanishing traces of Christ's presence.

Disenchanted by the creation's stubbornness, perhaps God gave up and quit.

Is this what the apostle Paul taught? Listen to him as he instructs the Colossians: "For in him all things in heaven and on earth were created, things visible and invisible, whether thrones or dominions or rulers or powers—all things have been created through him and for him" (Col. 1:16, NRSV). According to Paul, Christ not only created the universe but also made all the essential social orders. So the social institutions in which we live are parts of God's creation too. As a Hebrew who understood the importance of social contexts, Paul insisted that the social orders, as well as the physical universe, are fundamentally related to Christ's creative work ("through him and for him").

But perhaps this is no longer true. We know from the Gospel of John that God created the world through His Son (John 1:1-5). But maybe He grew weary of His world. Disenchanted by the creation's stubbornness, perhaps God gave up and quit. Perhaps now He's just awaiting an opportunity to hold a fire sale and then leave.

Many Christians today believe this. When stating their understanding of the Christian faith, they celebrate the world's demise.[2] The apostle Paul would not join in their celebrations! No statement in Paul's writings regarding Christ's relationship to the world is more stunning than the following: "In him all things hold together" (Col. 1:17). As both the world's originating and continuing cause, the gracious Christ is *right now* the world's reason for cohesion. At this very moment He is the reason there is *cosmos* and not *chaos*. Physicists study the order in basic atomic structure. Biologists ponder the intricacies of cellular structures. Astronomers observe the majesty of the universe. All of these result from the current activity of Christ the Creator (cf. Isa. 45:18-19).

If Paul is correct, then no one can speak despairingly of the world without speaking despairingly of Christ. To the extent that God's creation serves as sin's cabin boy, it does so as an unwilling slave, as one *kidnapped. Hope,* not despair; *sonship,* not slavery; *redemption,* not damnation, are creation's future.

Hope? Sonship? Redemption? Aren't such terms normally reserved for expressing the Christian gospel? Don't they apply to people only? Are they not used carelessly if applied to the world?

Because Paul understood the full scope of Christ's atonement, he insisted that not until the terms of redemption are applied to creation has the gospel been rightly spoken and believed. Moreover, not until one realizes that creation is fully included in the provisions of Christ's redemption can one properly live the holy

life. Otherwise, a person hobbles along with a constricted understanding of what sanctification includes.

Paul's writings support the idea that we should treat the
world as our fellow heir in Christ. In the Epistle to the Romans
(8:18-25) we learn that creation is now expectantly awaiting redemption in Christ, *even as we are.* The world is an inheritor of
grace, *even as we are.* In so many words, Paul tells us that creation
was pressed to serve sin's interests, just as the ship's captain
turned the honorable Robert Balfour into a slave. But slavery and
service to sin are neither the world's truth nor its future. Redemption draws nigh for creation, even as it does for us.

As a woman who is in labor, creation is waiting with eager
expectation for the revealing of the children of God (Rom. 8:19).
The joyous secret we Christians share
with the creation is that it "will be set
free from its bondage to decay and
will obtain the freedom of the glory of
the children of God" (v. 21, NRSV).
Christ will redeem the world from the
consequences of Adam's disobedience
(5:15-21). We and the creation share a
mutual promise, hope, and inheritance. And those who can hear the
voice of the Spirit of God will also be
able to hear the pained voice of creation longing for its redemption. Creation, the Spirit, and humanity. To-

> *Creation, the Spirit,
> and humanity.
> Together we form
> a chorus of groanings
> that sing out
> Christian hope.*

gether we form a chorus of groanings that sing out Christian
hope. For hope is central to creation's existence just as it is to
ours. The "living hope" about which Peter speaks (1 Pet. 1:3) belongs to creation too. If Paul is correct, then both the world and
we are being redeemed together, through the atoning work of
Christ. One will not be fulfilled apart from the other. As stewards who know the truth, Christians should help give voice to
the world's hope.

Anyone who attempts to defraud creation of its inheritance in
the kingdom of God should be aware that he or she is acting in
clear violation of God's Word. Efforts to make the kingdom of

grace safe by reducing its range have threatened the Church repeatedly. For many Christians, embracing what the apostle says in Romans will mean reversing years of contrary instruction. Sadly, in much of Evangelical Christianity the notion that the world has no inheritance in the kingdom of God has become fixed dogma. The error is celebrated in songs and sermons.

When the Kingdom is consummated, creation's truth will be revealed for all to see. At the revealing of the Son of Man in glory (Dan. 7:22, 27; 12:1-3; Luke 12:32; 22:28-30; Rom. 5:17; 1 Cor. 6:2-3), creation will be present as a triumphant participant (Rom. 8:19). In the meantime, Christians should *now* show their awareness of creation's inheritance and future. They should do so by the way they treat the world and by how they live in relationship to it. Clearly, we Christians should relate to creation in much the same way we do others who are being redeemed by God's grace. By the grace of Christ, both we and creation are living toward God's future.

> *Who should love the world more than a Christian?*

We can no more wait until the Kingdom's consummation to begin treating creation like a child of God than we can wait until then to begin living a holy life. The realized promises associated with the Kingdom's inauguration apply to creation now as surely as they apply to us. Our witness to the gospel of Christ will include our relationship to the world.

A holy life is one that suffers with Christ (Phil. 3:10; 1 Pet. 4:13). It is also one that suffers with suffering creation. Christians are called to act as compassionate friends toward their world, suffering for it in anticipation of better times. Who should love the world more than a Christian?

Second, let's look at Christ's assessment of creation. Jesus' life provides us two examples. The *first* is the Incarnation. Among the best words creation ever heard were "And the Word became flesh" (John 1:14, RSV). This creation hosted the holy God! In a virgin mother's womb, in a cattle stall, and on a donkey's back, *God was with us.* Furthermore, by becoming incarnate in human flesh, God didn't jeopardize His deity at all. Instead,

He used creation to reveal himself most completely. Unquestionably, God has embraced His creation. He has told us the truth about the world. It can be, and will be, redeemed.

The *second* example from Christ's life that teaches us to treat the world as a fellow pilgrim is the sacrament of the Lord's Supper. When Jesus took the bread, blessed it, and broke it for the disciples, He showed how even the most common of foods can be elevated in significance to express the depths of God's love. Then, by taking the cup, blessing it, and giving it to the disciples, Jesus used a common drink of the day to articulate the ultimate expression of divine self-giving. We call the bread and the wine "sacraments" because the Almighty God of the universe selected ordinary elements of the creation and human life and transformed them into transparent vehicles for revealing himself to us.

Bread and wine were common. Ordinary people used them daily. They were the ingredients of life. When choosing symbols through which to express clearly what God's love means, Christ chose the common, not the exquisite. He chose elements that could easily represent the whole creation. No one need be embarrassed in the presence of bread and wine. Christ demonstrated that no part of creation is excluded as a potential vehicle for divine self-disclosure.

The Sacramental Significance of the Secular

After what Christ did with the bread and the wine, can there be any doubt about creation's significance? The Lord's Supper graces creation as it has never been graced before. It proclaims that God and creation are now inseparably joined. He has enlisted it in the service of proclamation.

From the Lord's Supper onward, the world must be viewed as more than just common or secular. The whole creation has now received a sacramental assignment. The world becomes an instrument for declaring the name of the Lord.

Even our vocations become vehicles through which the world can be sanctified. God takes the stuff of life, blesses it, breaks it, and uses it for declaring His righteous name among the nations. The Lord's Supper has taught us that God can use the world—including our jobs—to fulfill the purposes of holy love.

In all places there are Christians who treat their vocations sacramentally, using them as a means for showing that the world belongs to God. They are convinced that this world is God's object of redemption.

In Bridgeton, New Jersey, lives a woman named Sidna Prickett who owns Roarke Real Estate Agency.

"I'm in real estate because I'm a Christian," Sidna explains. "I see real estate as a wonderful opportunity to serve God by serving others. I view the marketplace sacramentally." Sidna carries out this vision daily. "Repeatedly I use my skills as a Realtor to act justly and mercifully toward elderly persons who are in danger of losing their homes," she says. "I do the same for divorced mothers who are without adequate housing. I know how to work with programs that will benefit the poor, and I help them find affordable housing. For me, all of this is an intentional act of worship."

Sidna thinks God is acting redemptively toward His creation through her. "More and more I see how He uses me to weave a tapestry of justice and mercy in my small part of the world."

In Little Rock, Arkansas, Daniel Holom is vice president, investments, Morgan Stanley Dean Witter Discover. Daniel has thought a lot about what sacramental living should look like. He says, "I think of my vocation as my parish in the world of investments. I believe God is acting redemptively in the world and that I'm one of His instruments.

"This might sound corny, but the way I conduct my affairs as a stockbroker is itself part of my witness. I also want to establish a lifetime relationship with each client. In my business, growth is the driving force. But many times I have turned down growth because I knew that particular purchases would not be good for my clients. I want the world of stock investments to be marked by integrity at every turn, and I must be a means through which that happens."

Integrity, Daniel says, is the vehicle being used to make his vocation sacramental in nature: "I believe that integrity characterizes the gospel. Accordingly, I treat my profession sacramentally by making Christian integrity the controlling principle of all I do. God will redeem His creation partly through integrity in the world of investments."

Helen Kannady lives in Tulsa, Oklahoma. For 17 years she

worked as an attorney, seven of which she served as a juvenile judge for the District Court of Tulsa County. In that assignment she had to deal with the reality of a disintegrating social fabric.

Helen says that she served as a judge because she knew it to be God's will. Service on the bench was a means by which she could express the integrity and hope Christ had given to her. Helen speaks freely of her belief that the grace of God was at work in even the worst of cases brought before her. "My responsibility was to identify the glimmers of God's grace through which I could try to act redemptively," she says. The incarnation of hope, of trying to find the good and to build upon it, marked Helen's tenure as a judge.

Helen recalls one particular mother and delinquent son who appeared before her. The mother verbally accosted her before she could speak: "Who do you think you are? You sit on that bench in your security and black robe!" the distraught mother said sharply. "You have no idea how difficult it is to raise a son in a bad neighborhood when you're poor and a single mother!"

Judge Kannady could have had the mother arrested for contempt of court. Instead, she cleared the courtroom of everyone except herself and the angry mother. Then Helen removed her judge's robe, placed it on her chair, came down, and sat beside the mother. "You're correct," Helen said. "I don't understand your world as you do. Now—together let's solve this problem and help your son."

Howard defines politics as "the art of securing and maintaining a principled peace among persons with conflicting values and interests."

One hundred miles southwest of Tulsa lies Oklahoma City. Among the legislators who make the laws for Oklahoma is Senator Howard Hendricks, Senate District 52. Howard has been a member of the Oklahoma State Legislature since 1988. Holding a standard of justice, mercy, and peace is the reason he is in politics. Howard speaks of his office as a vehicle through which to glorify God in the world. He believes that human structures can be made serviceable to God, in that sense *sanctified,* although he doesn't mean that the powers of state should be used to force Christianity on others.

Howard defines politics as "the art of securing and maintaining a principled peace among persons with conflicting values and interests." What is the sacramental quality of Howard's service as a public servant?

"As a Christian who bears witness to the Creator God," he explains, "I'm there as one who works to secure and maintain a principled peace in the midst of a morally bent world. Seeking a position of public trust and responsibility is every bit as much a calling for me as that experienced by a Christian minister."

Theologian Hendrikus Berkhof would say that Howard Hendricks is sanctifying the secular. As a Christian, he is trying to transform the structures of society so that they will allow more scope and greater effectiveness for the deeds of love.[3]

Susanna Fitzgerald is a clinical social worker and psychotherapist. "In my early years as a Christian, I was not taught to view the world sacramentally," Susanna says. "The world was excluded from the scope of redemption. But my perception of God's world has changed."

As a psychotherapist, Susanna regularly encounters persons who have been deeply wounded by their pasts. She knows the damage that distorted life contexts can do to persons and families. "But," she says, "hope, not despair, is the way I approach the world. I think of my profession in sacramental terms. I believe that in small ways I'm a redemptive agent through which the grace of God moves to transform the world."

For Susanna, sacramental living in the world means "being Jesus with skin—a source of hope amidst apparent hopelessness."

"I'm aware of the sacramental quality attached to uncovering and healing the wounds that have crippled persons and families," she says.

The sanctification of the world occurs between the *already* and the *not yet.* The kingdom of God has been inaugurated in Christ. Already it is among us (Luke 17:20-21). By God's grace we have entered it. Today, not in some distant future, sanctification of the secular begins. The parable of the wise and foolish stewards directly applies to our responsibility (Luke 19:11-27). As the stewards waited for the ruler to return, they were supposed to invest carefully all the master had entrusted to them. Only the foolish steward wrapped his portion in a piece of cloth and hid it.

Our responsibility to invest is urgent, yet the parable also teaches that some components of stewardship cannot be completed until the Nobleman returns. Only then will the kingdom of God come in its fullness. Christians can live confidently in the knowledge that the Kingdom *has* come. This is the *ground* for sacramental living. And we live confidently in the knowledge that the Kingdom *will* come. This is the *horizon* for sacramental living. The sanctification of the world that has begun will be completed (Col. 1:20; Rev. 11:15). Living sacramentally and redemptively in relationship to the world is our privilege and responsibility.

We pray for the coming of God's everlasting kingdom, this kingdom of glory which is the continuation and perfection of the kingdom of grace on earth.

—John Wesley
Sermon: "Sermon on the Mount"

The writings in the Old and New Testaments comprise the history book of God's promises. The Bible tells the story of God's hope which will be fulfilled in the whole world. . . . It recounts the past in such a way that through it a new future and freedom for the hearers is inaugurated.

—Jurgen Moltmann
The Experiment Hope

Our divine future is present with us through the Word: The final reality purposed for us by God is [now] present.

—Karl Barth
The Holy Spirit and the Christian Life

CHAPTER 13

A Dangerous Hope

IN CHAPTER 3 WE DISCUSSED THE SIN OF ADAM IN TURN-ing to the creation as the source of life and object of ultimate value. By taking the fruit, he turned away from God's person and promises as though they were not enough for living securely. Instead, Adam's actions implied, this created world can offer a more firm hope for making human life secure. Adam tried to place the created order, including humanity, in God's position. That was his sin.

We also said in the third chapter that Adam's sin was primarily one of "unfaith." Even though created in God's own image, Adam refused to worship and trust God. He rejected the role God had planned for him. He was to have been God's special steward in the whole creation. By trusting God, Adam was to have shown just who God is and what the world was supposed to be. Instead, he bought the tempter's lie and turned to the creation as his primary reason for living. Adam said in effect, "I am no more than an animal, and all that I *am* can be satisfied as the animals are." As a result, he "did not honor [God] or give thanks to him, but . . . became futile in [his] thinking" (Rom. 1:21, NRSV). Both Genesis and the first chapter of Romans detail what happened when humanity followed in Adam's train.

When by the Holy Spirit's enlightenment we reflect upon humanity's "lost estate," the tragedy overwhelms us. The impact is compounded every time we hear of one more rape, one more political scandal, one more case of child abuse. No wonder Christians are called upon to suffer with Christ in this broken world. Dare we hope for anything more?

Humanity as the Creature Who Hopes

Why does creation, including the things we humans have fabricated, hold such an attraction for us? Why would humanity turn from God as the primary source of life and meaning? How is it that with our whole person we could walk away from the Creator and attach the significance of deity to the things God created? *Part* of the answer lies in the way we confront our finitude, our painfully apparent vulnerability in the world.[1]

One of the obvious characteristics of what it means to be human is not only that we are finite but also that we can reflect upon, ponder, our finitude. Even at elementary levels, we recognize our impermanence. We think about, sing about, and write poems about our mortality. When we pass a cemetery or meet a funeral procession, most of us spend at least a moment thinking of our own eventual death. A visit to a nursing home prompts similar considerations. For some people, consideration of mortality becomes so disruptive they commit suicide.

Finite? No doubt. But we humans are far more than that. We know we share biological similarities and dependencies with animals. The medicines we depend upon that were first tested in mice illustrate this. The Bible states bluntly that we were made "from the dust of the ground" (Gen. 2:7). But we are also profoundly aware that "dust of the ground" doesn't exhaust who we are.

No one can ever successfully reduce the human person to the natural order that contains rabbits and elephants. There is another dimension to being human. Unique among the creation, we were created in the image of God. The human record consistently shows that we yearn for the transcendent, the divine, the eternal. We know that we have capacities for creativity, for community, for love, and for meaning that come directly from God, not from the dust of the ground. The universal human record demonstrates that we spend a lot of time reflecting on this dimension of personhood too.

Made for the earth? Yes. But we were also made for You, O God, for splendid communion with You. We were made by You, for life with You, in this world where You have placed us. We have been created in Your image, O God, and we cannot rest apart from You!

In the modern era there have been many unsuccessful efforts

to reduce human life to the material. We have been told by famous people that what we believe to be our kinship with the divine is best explained on purely biological, psychological, and sociological grounds. Karl Marx, Friedrich Nietzsche, and Sigmund Freud, among others, have tried to talk us out of our conviction that we are fundamentally oriented toward the eternal God. In the end, they have told us, after all the religions have written their scriptures, and after all the hymnists have sung their songs, the final, cold curtain of death comes down on it all. The physiological, socio-logical, and psychological systems shut down, and we die. This has been part of the "gospel" of secularism in the mod-ern era.

Tired of endless attempts to reduce it to insignificance, the human spirit finally stands up and says . . . "I am more!"

But secularism has failed on a grand scale. Not because obstinate Jews and Christians have disagreed, but be-cause, finally, the human spirit rejected it. Tired of endless attempts to reduce it to insignificance, the human spirit final-ly stands up and says to the secularist, "I am more!" At about the time secularism was ready to conduct a wake for religion, along came the New Age movement and other bursts of religious hunger. Composed largely of the intellectual elite who were sup-posed to have been the disciples of secularism, these new move-ments have voiced a pent-up yearning for transcendence. As much as Christians might look askance at the New Age movement, this much is clear: it demonstrates humanity's unquenchable kinship with and hunger for God. We can now see more clearly than ever that the modern effort to dissolve the human spirit into the natural order was an abject failure. The debris of that effort lie wrecked and bleaching on many shores.

Yes, we are very much sociological, biological, psychological, and economic creatures. Because of the natural and social sciences, we now understand this more than ever before. But none of those factors can provide fundamental insight into the human spirit. On-ly the Genesis statement can do that: "So God created man in his own image, in the image of God he created him; male and female he created them" (1:27, RSV). This is what the Bible affirms, and this is what the long human record of peoples and nations confirm. The contention that we are simply "animals who make tools" collapses before our unquenchable thirst for the divine. Our own hunger and our own poetic and cultural creativity confirm that we are created in God's image. We can never be fully human apart from fellowship with Him.

Among all God's creatures, humanity is the one who is richly endowed with the ability to hope. In one sense, we are human *because* we can hope. Hope grows out of our special location in creation. If we were no more than beetles, there would be no reason to hope. And if the meaning we generate as humans were in no way threatened, there would be no *need* to hope. But we do hope because we generate meaning, though we are surrounded by many factors that threaten that meaning.

Adam and all his children have hoped and misplaced hope. As humans, we long for something that will give sufficient and secure meaning to our unique and wonderful existence. But the Bible affirms and our human experience bears witness that creation itself simply cannot carry that weight. It cannot provide what the tempter promised Adam so long ago. Life according to the flesh results in death every time (Rom. 5:12-14).

Is there a hope, a sure source for meaning, that does not remove us from our humanity? Does the meaning we generate through our homes, occupations, churches, and recreation have any place in God? Or is the human arena just a cruel, superficial illusion after all? Dare we hold fast to the dangerous hope that we can worship and commune with God—really know Him, *smack in the middle* of our finitude?

Humanity as a Creator of Fragile Meaning

Let's consider our complexity as persons and the importance of human meaning. After each creative event recorded in Genesis, during which God brought forth the natural order, there followed a divine assessment: "And God saw that it was good" (1:12, 18, 21, 25). God's assessment of His creation forever separates the Judeo-Christian tradition from philosophies and religions that view the

world as an obstacle to human fulfillment. Nowhere does God re-
tract His assessment of His creation. Anyone who wants to walk in
God's story must come to grips with the goodness of finitude.

In this world, as marvelous combinations of the natural and
the transcendent, we humans give birth to complex cultures
through which we create, express, guard, and transmit meaning.
We shape values (meaning) and are shaped by them. This is a part
of our stewardship and greatness. American pioneers, for example,
turned trees into villages that housed churches, schools, and busi-
nesses. Throughout our history we have generated meaning
through art, music, family, entertainment, and our economic structures. We think about values, discuss them, institutionalize them,
and seek to transmit them. Sometimes values are fairly incidental,
having no broad impact on society. At other times religious, moral,
and economic values have profound influence upon the shapes of
cultures and the people who inhabit
them. This cycle of generating values
and transmitting them to others, creating cultures and giving them stability
through institutions, was anticipated
and endorsed by God when He created
us. Through this creative process God
could be glorified and worshiped. The
process of being human, of being a
steward, in this world is an appropriate
vehicle for worshiping God.

*We are aware
of the fact that
try as we might,
we may not be
here tomorrow.*

An important part of what it means
to be human is our *awareness* of how fragile these structures of
meaning are. We are aware of the fact that try as we might, we may
not be here tomorrow. We know that many spheres of meaning in
our lives are quite vulnerable. A person who learns abruptly that
his or her spouse wants to end a marriage knows all too well how
fragile life can be. In such times the naked vulnerability of our
flimsy hold on meaning becomes overwhelming. We hope for a
center of meaning that can hold us even when other meanings are
being shaken. If we could not hope in this way, we would not be
human.

The fundamental problem we humans face with regard to

hope is that we have focused our hope in the wrong place. We have attached ultimate significance to things just as vulnerable as we are: what people think of us, how we perform at work—the list could go on and on. What did the tempter offer Adam and Eve? Just more "nature"? One little apple? Oh, no. Sin is never this simple. It's far more subtle and tragic. The tempter claimed to offer Adam and Eve a *better way* to insure meaning than God could offer. In so many words he said, "If you really want to secure your shaky grasp on meaning, turn to creation. Trust it. It will never fail you. Take in as much as you can. It will fulfill you."

Hope is not something God tacked on at the end of the gospel.

Adam quickly signed on the dotted line. He didn't even consult God about his decision—he bought the lie. *And so have we, every one of us.* The Word of God declares it, and our individual and corporate histories confirm it: "All, both Jews and Greeks, are under the power of sin" (Rom. 3:9, NRSV).

Was the tempter correct? Not if scarred civilizations, individuals, families, and lands offer reliable evidence. Not if the anxiety and failure that dog our endless efforts to find fulfillment in material promises can be trusted. Our culture daily exposes the sin and futility of trying to find hope and human meaning in such pursuits. But on we rush. Surely success lies around the next turn. Undoubtedly one more drink of greed, one more morsel of deceit, and we'll be satisfied. Life according to the flesh.

The Bible maintains, and the human record confirms it, "Sin, when it is fully grown, gives birth to death" (James 1:15, NRSV). Sin simply doesn't deliver what the tempter's contract promised: a basis for hope. Finally, all efforts to anchor the human spirit in the finite rather than in God collapse. It could not have been otherwise.

The Gospel of Hope

The Christian faith is no stranger to hope. Hope is at the center of the gospel of the crucified and resurrected Christ (1 Pet. 1:3). Some would say Christians live dangerously. Putting all their eggs in one basket. Daring to believe that in the gospel alone there is an adequate ground for human meaning. Daring to believe that the gospel of hope is addressed to human life in all its dimensions. Knowing that otherwise the gospel would not really be good news.

Hope is not something God tacked on at the end of the gospel. The gospel doesn't just talk *about* hope. It *is* hope. In the gospel of grace, the goodness of our humanity is clarified and made secure. Through Christ, life can once again be centered in the Creator instead of creation. The whole of life can be entrusted to God through Jesus Christ. "Come to me, all who labor and are heavy laden, and I will give you rest" (Matt. 11:28, RSV), Jesus said. "If you knew the gift of God . . . you would have asked him, and he would have given you living water" (John 4:10, RSV), He exhorted the Samaritan woman. "I am the resurrection and the life" (John 11:25), He promised the grieving Martha. The apostle Paul puts it beautifully from another perspective: "For God . . . sending his own Son in the likeness of sinful flesh and for sin, he condemned sin in the flesh, in order that the just requirement of the law might be fulfilled in us, who walk not according to the flesh but according to the Spirit" (Rom. 8:3-4, RSV).

> *Right here, in the arena where we, along with Adam, bought the lie, the gospel of hope reaches us.*

Where does this "walking according to the Spirit" that Paul talks about occur? Right here in the created order that God called good. *In* the flesh, *by* the Spirit. This is the promise of the gospel of Jesus Christ, and it is the hope for human meaning.

The gospel is good news for us because it's good news about God. He is with us now and will be with us forever (Rev. 1:4). Our future is as secure as God himself.

Because of the cross and resurrection of Jesus, Christians know that there is every good reason to trust in God and not in powers or principalities. By the power of God in our Lord's resurrection, He prevailed over death and hell, over the strongest powers of chaos and evil. "He disarmed the rulers and authorities and made a public example of them, triumphing over them in [the Cross]" (Col. 2:15, NRSV). All that Jesus accomplished He now through the

Holy Spirit gives to His brothers and sisters (John 16:12-15; Col. 2:8-15).

God lifts His children above this world's dependence on itself. He liberates us from the powers of darkness that want to claim us as their own and set limits on our hope. In His resurrection Christ anchors our hope, our meaning, our existence. Christ alone is God's Alpha and Omega—the origin and the goal of hope (Rev. 21:5-6). He is the pivotal meaning that judges, organizes, and grounds all other meanings in life (Matt. 6:33).

Christ is God's good news for finite humankind and for this world in which we live. Right here, in the arena where we, along with Adam, bought the lie, the gospel of hope reaches us. It is active in the everyday stuff of life. The gospel has reached us in our successes and failures, and its content is hope.

Christians should live with a confidence that appears reckless to those who do not know Christ.

Christian hope does not rise or fall with the ups and downs of the time. We know that the salvation begun by our Lord will be completed. In the between time, Christians are aware of the powers that struggle against the advancing kingdom of God. We observe them at work every day and live amid their dangers. They disrupt families, exploit human sexuality, and twist personalities. They enslave people and corrupt institutions. Many Christians suffer directly because of the forces that oppose the gospel. Governments may oppress the Church. Entertainment media may try to denigrate Christians. Even family members sometimes persecute one another. Living *in* Christian faith and *by* Christian convictions is definitely risky business.

Christians also suffer *with* the world. No one feels more pain than Christians when wars leave children orphaned, turn wives into widows, slaughter soldiers, and ravage nations. We should suffer with the world because we see the discrepancy between what God intends for His creation and what sin does to distort it. We also suffer expectantly because we see *what is* and we know *what will be* when the Kingdom comes in its fullness (Rom. 8:20-22).

One characteristic of Christian hope is that it provides strength to act (2 Cor. 3:12-18). Christians should live with a confidence that appears reckless to those who do not know Christ. The apostle Paul prayed that "the God of hope" would fill the Roman Christians with "all joy and peace in believing" (15:13, RSV). He wanted them to abound in hope. We know from Paul's Epistles that in spite of all his afflictions, he lived this way. The apostle Peter sounds the same note: "Therefore gird up your minds, be sober, set your hope fully upon the grace that is coming to you at the revelation of Jesus Christ" (1 Pet. 1:13, RSV). Living in hope will inspire in us obedience to God, commitment to holy living, and courage tempered by caution (1 Pet. 1:14-17).

Another important characteristic of Christian hope is that it gives birth to peace and joy. Paul prays that the God of hope will fill the Roman Christians with "all joy and peace in believing" (Rom. 15:13, RSV). Jesus said to His disciples, "Peace [shalom in Hebrew] I leave with you; my peace I give to you; not as the world gives do I give to you. Let not your hearts be troubled, neither let them be afraid" (John 14:27, RSV). Writers of the Epistles often extend the peace of God, or the peace of Christ, to their readers (Rom. 1:7; 1 Cor. 1:3; Gal. 1:3; 1 Pet. 1:2; 2 John 3).

In the Bible the word "peace" implies harmony, wholeness, rest, integrity, and tranquillity. The world cannot give the peace of God, because it doesn't have the permanence, authority, and stability needed to anchor peace. The false sense of security the world offers is always plagued by the threat of disruption. Only God can give real peace. His shalom encircles those who know Him and live in Him.

Because God can give real peace, He can also give real joy. Jesus promised His disciples that His joy would remain in them and that their joy would be full (John 15:11). No one, Jesus said, can take His joy from His disciples (16:22). The apostle Paul explains that Christian joy is to "rejoice in God" (Rom. 5:11), a joy that comes because we have been reconciled to the Heavenly Father through Christ. Peace with God brings joy. For Paul, these two characterize the nature of the Kingdom. "For the kingdom of God is not food and drink but righteousness and peace and joy in the Holy Spirit" (Rom. 14:17, RSV).

The peace and joy that characterize Christian hope are not circumstantial. In fact, often in the New Testament peace and joy are celebrated in the midst of extremely undesirable circumstances. Paul said to the Thessalonian Christians, "For you received the word in much affliction, with joy inspired by the Holy Spirit" (1 Thess. 1:6, RSV). Jesus himself, of course, is the greatest example of this. The author of Hebrews urged his readers to emulate Christ, "the pioneer and perfecter of our faith, who for the joy that was set before him endured the cross, despising the shame" (12:2, RSV).

In a time when blind leaders of the blind are hawking prosperity, happiness, and earthly well-being as the equivalent of Christian peace and joy, it becomes all the more important to discriminate between the authentic and the counterfeit. The truth is that real peace and joy are joined only to Christian hope.

Living in the Gospel of Hope

Christians must be people who live according to the gospel of hope. The ways in which we relate to God's creation should be noticeably different from those of unbelievers. Unless that happens, the gospel of hope loses its appeal to the lost world around us.

Living in Christian hope is holy living. The apostle Peter asked a question that included its own answer: "What sort of persons ought you to be in lives of holiness and godliness, waiting for and hastening the coming of the day of God" (2 Pet. 3:11-12, RSV). Hope sanctifies all of life by centering it in the kingdom of God. This doesn't mean for one moment that our vocations and responsibilities in the world lose their importance. To the contrary, they take on a new importance by finding their proper focus and service. Hope transforms our finite life without in any way diminishing it.

Christian hope makes possible an active and confident life of holiness.

Christian hope makes possible an active and confident life of holiness. It addresses the powers and principalities, not in fear, but in certainty and in the power of the Spirit (Eph. 6:12-17). For the kingdoms of this world are becoming the kingdoms of our Lord, "and he will reign for ever and ever" (Rev. 11:15). When we are firmly anchored in Christian hope, we can live with the authority that Kingdom life offers. Christian hope accounts for the tone of certainty the New Testament Epistles exhibit. They were written in circumstances that would have normally generated despair. That did not happen. The one book in the New Testament given completely to Christian hope, Revelation, was written by a man the Romans had banished to an island prison. Good news—the resurrected Christ who empowered our brothers and sisters for confident living so long ago is with us now.

The writer to the Hebrews urges his hearers "to seize the hope set before us" (6:18, RSV). German theologian Jurgen Moltmann echoes the sentiment: "'It is written' will become 'it has taken place.' Some day, in nature, in history, and in society, we will no longer encounter temptations and contradictions, but confirmation of what has been promised. Some day, promise and reality, hope and experience will be in accord."[2]

Until then, Moltmann says, we should live the Christian hope. And hope will be more real than all the promises and ambiguities offered by the present age. We will put our trust in God—in the riches He has assigned to us in Christ, through the Spirit—rather than in the created order. Until the Kingdom comes in its fullness, the Church should be a community in which hope is celebrated and practiced.

Let the Church be a people that heralds the gospel of true hope in this world so pitifully broken by false hope. Let the Church live in the hope that advances the kingdom of God in His good creation. Let there be holy living through the meaning and power of the gospel. May we be people who live in, and live out, the dangerous Christian hope by placing all of life in the gospel's promises. And may we live under the Holy Spirit's comprehensive cleansing, empowerment, and governance. Amen.

EPILOGUE

Our journey together started when the authors asked us to join a *focus group* for a book they were writing. Their plan was to involve six Nazarenes in *focusing* with purpose and specificity on the book's content. Our assignment was to read carefully, critique candidly, and discuss openly the manuscript, chapter by chapter, as it was written.

Not fully grasping what we would encounter, we signed on for the trip. After receiving the first three chapters by mail, we met on a frigid, January evening at the Truesdale residence for our first face-to-face appointment with the authors. As we took time to become acquainted, we learned that we were a diverse and eclectic group. Gender: two females and four males. Age: 26 to 59. Education: high school diploma to graduate degrees. Vocation: business executive, counselor, editor, school administrator, pastor, and data analyst. Church background: four Wesleyans and two Calvinists. We decided that if the authors wanted different perspectives, they certainly chose the participants well.

From that first meeting, it was obvious that the group was *focused* and that we would meld. All of us were captivated by the topic, "sanctification," and we were delighted with the thread of *grace* that was woven into the book's fabric.

We discovered that the authors, Al and Bonnie, were incredible to work with. How comfortable they were to accept our straightforward comments and evaluation of the book! They were willing to take risks as they allowed us to examine and question and probe. *Rather extraordinary,* we thought.

So, our journey began. And what a journey it has been! The more times we met, sometimes monthly and sometimes more frequently, the more we realized that our assessment in January was correct. The authors were genuine in their desire to write a book that would communicate to *thinking* laypersons, to those who sincerely wanted to explore and study the doctrine of entire sanctification. Al and Bonnie were willing to speak "our language." This would not be a theological treatise penned by theologians for other theologians. It would serve well the reflective, probing, inquiring mind of any believer.

As we journeyed, we made countless stops along the way. We

would often discuss, deliberate, explore, query, and debate for hours at a time. We also found our three-hour sessions were usually inadequate to fully consider a single chapter. Yet, in spite of our diversity, we discovered we were in agreement and harmony with the concepts and truths of the text. A highlight of each meeting was sharing our *ah-has*—those precious nuggets in the book that spoke to us in special ways. Often we left the Truesdales' home with a mix of emotions—frustration and perplexity, satisfaction and fulfillment. We always went away in a reflective mood with much to mentally massage, not just for days but for weeks and months—and maybe for the rest of our lives.

But how has our journey gone? Has the commitment of six months of our lives made a difference? Have there been any significant changes in our minds and hearts? Permit us to briefly share a bit of the growth that has occurred in our lives.

The one word that best describes the transformation within us is *freedom*. We found the entire journey *freeing* as we examined and questioned the manuscript. Then we rejoiced and celebrated as we made new discoveries. What freedom we experienced through the half-year journey! Freedom from our pasts. Freedom from misconceptions. Freedom from erroneous teaching. Freedom from ongoing struggles. Freedom to confess. Freedom to hope. Freedom to live in sanctifying grace. What marvelous, incomparable freedom!

We can summarize our growth in three very profound ways:

1. We have come to realize fully what the authors mean by the statement: "Sanctification means putting all of life in the stream of God's transforming grace." We are now living in the "stream of grace" as never before. This stream is giving us a new freedom as God's sanctifying grace works within us—cleansing, liberating, and empowering. This new freedom has opened to us the realm of the *cans*, not the *can'ts*, of the Kingdom. The stream of transforming grace is allowing us to see clearly what our faith *can* do rather than being blinded by the limitations of the *can'ts*. What freedom!

2. We have come to appreciate and accept gratefully the authors' declaration: "The grace of God sets us free from the tyranny of perfection, and that is good news." For all of us, but especially those with a Wesleyan heritage, we learned that we shared a common experience as youth. Though ministers and teachers were well-inten-

tioned, their holiness message, it seemed to us, emphasized the wrath and judgment of God rather than His love and grace. Consequently, we struggled for years and years with the concept of Christian perfection and God's impending fury because we weren't "perfect." But the good news is that God's grace frees us from this tyranny. Fighting-type words are now eliminated from our vocabulary. The struggle is over. Hallelujah! What glorious freedom!

3. We have come to value and treasure the authors' proclamation: "The Christian doctrine of sanctification requires a sturdy balance between the *already* and the *not yet.*" We realize that we began the journey into Christ at the same place when He chose us and we accepted His gift of salvation. Yet our individual histories result in our travels on the Christian walk at various rates. Likewise, the six of us entered our journey with Al and Bonnie at different places because of our own histories, and we leave the journey at diverse junctures. But each of us understands that we are somewhere between the *already* and the *not yet.* We were when we started this jaunt at the beginning of 1996, and we still are several months later. As we dealt with a couple of the chapters, we grappled with the material, and still are. All of our questions have not been satisfactorily answered—yet. As Al and Bonnie remind us: "Christian discipleship is an *inaugurated* and *unending* journey into God's transforming grace." This, to us, is freedom. Wonderful, amazing freedom!

Today, we're rejoicing and celebrating in our new discoveries. We're living and working *sacramentally,* endeavoring to be the *redemptive agents* that God and this book challenges us to be. And that is our prayer for you. Through your careful reading and rereading, your diligent study, and your never-ending quest, may you find in these pages new truths and understandings about the glorious doctrine of sanctification. We encourage you to journey with us by putting your life in the stream of this transforming, life-changing, freedom-giving grace. You'll be glad you did. Guaranteed.

Dan Braaten
Wes Eby
Susanna Fitzgerald
Mike Oyster
Sandra Parks
Rex Perry

APPENDIX

The Apostles' Creed

I believe in God the Father Almighty,
Maker of heaven and earth;

And in Jesus Christ, His only Son, our Lord;
who was conceived by the Holy Spirit,
born of the Virgin Mary,
suffered under Pontius Pilate,
was crucified, dead, and buried;
He descended into hades;
the third day He rose again from the dead;
He ascended into heaven,
and sitteth at the right hand of God the Father Almighty;
from thence he shall come to judge the living and the dead.

I believe in the Holy Spirit,
the Church universal,
the communion of saints,
the forgiveness of sins,
the resurrection of the body,
and the life everlasting.
Amen.

The Nicene Creed

I believe in one God the Father Almighty.
Maker of heaven and earth,
and of all things visible and invisible;

And in one Lord Jesus Christ,
the only-begotten Son of God,
begotten of His Father before all worlds,
God of God, Light of Light,
very God of very God,
begotten, not made,
being of one substance with the Father,
by whom all things were made;
who for us and for our salvation came down from heaven,
and was incarnate by the Holy Spirit of the Virgin Mary,
and was made man,
and crucified also for us under Pontius Pilate;
He suffered and was buried,
and the third day He rose again according to the Scriptures,
and ascended into heaven,
and sitteth on the right hand of the Father;
and He shall come again with glory to judge both the living and the dead;
whose kingdom shall have no end.

And I believe in the Holy Spirit,
the Lord and Giver of life,
who proceedeth from the Father and the Son,
who with the Father and the Son together is worshiped and glorified;
who spoke by the prophets.

And I believe in one universal and apostolic church;
I acknowledge one baptism for the remission of sins;
and I look for the resurrection of the dead,
and the life of the world to come.
Amen.

Notes

Chapter 1

1. *Reader's Digest*, November 1991, 78-80.
2. Gustaf Aulén, *The Faith of the Christian Church* (Minneapolis: Fortress Press, 1960), 102.
3. Erich Fromm, *You Shall Be as Gods* (Chicago: Holt, Rinehart, and Winston, 1966), 179.

Chapter 2

1. Elie Wiesel, *The Kingdom of Memory: Reminiscences* (New York: Summit Books, 1990), 156.

Chapter 4

1. Martin Luther, The Large Catechism, (1529) *Luther's Primary Works,* ed. Henry Ware and C. A. Buchheim (London: Hodder and Stoughton, 1896).
2. Annie Dillard, *Pilgrim at Tinker Creek* (New York: Harper Perennial, 1988), 269-70.

Chapter 5

1. Flannery O'Connor, *A Good Man Is Hard to Find and Other Short Stories* (New York: Harcourt, Brace, and World, Inc., 1955), 28.

Chapter 6

1. Karl Barth, *The Holy Spirit and the Christian Life* (Louisville, Ky.: Westminster/John Knox Press, 1993), 29.
2. Ibid., 32.
3. Karl Barth, *Dogmatics in Outlines* (New York: Harper and Row Publishers, 1959), 19.
4. Martin Luther, Sermon on John 3:16.
5. Martin Luther, "Concerning Christian Liberty," *Luther's Primary Works,* ed. Henry Wace (London: Hodder and Stoughton, 1896), 255-93.

Chapter 7

1. Lycurgus Starkey, *The Work of the Holy Spirit* (New York: Abingdon Press, 1962), 162.
2. Fyodor Dostoyevsky, *The Brothers Karamazov* (New York: The Modern Library, Book V, Section V), 255-73. First published in a Moscow magazine during 1879-1880.
3. Donald Bloeach, *God the Almighty* (Downers Grove, Ill.: Intervarsity Press, 1995), 158.
4. Sermon, "The Means of Grace," in *The Works of John Wesley*, 3rd ed., 14 vols. (London: Wesleyan Methodist Book Room 1872. Reprint, Kansas City: Beacon Hill Press of Kansas City, 1978), 5:200.
5. Sermon, "On Working Out Our Own Salvation," *The Works*, 102.

Chapter 8

1. While many observers believe that we have now entered a postmodern era, the modern era has placed its stamp on the Church and on us as Christians in identifiable

ways. The modern era began roughly around 1500. No sharp dividing line marks its beginning. Some of the distinguishing features of the modern era are the birth and maturation of modern science; the emergence of democratic philosophy and state making; mechanized technology; liberal philosophy regarding the rights of persons; capitalism; and denominationalism in America. Modernity affected how most of us think about religion, values, and the world. One characteristic of modernity is our belief that the existence and power of the state rests totally on the will and consent of the governed. Another characteristic, closely related to the first, is that the individual ego becoming the clearinghouse for deciding what is true and valuable in religion and morality. The ego became the bar before which claimants to truth must be assessed.

2. Stanley Hauerwas, *A Community of Character* (Notre Dame, Ind.: University of Notre Dame Press, 1981), 9.

3. "Modernity" simply designates human thought, practices, and institutions that have characterized the modern era. Increasingly, observers of Western society refer to the mid to late 20th century as marking the beginning of the postmodern era.

4. Michael Sandel, *Democracy's Discontent: America in Search of a Public Philosophy* (Cambridge, Mass.: Harvard University Press, 1996).

Chapter 9

1. Both of these creeds appear in the Appendix.

2. William M. Greathouse, "Holiness: Why All the Confusion?" *Herald of Holiness,* March 1996, 14.

3. The full text of the confession is located in John P. Bowen, "Japanese Church Seeks Reconciliation with Nazarenes in Korea," *World Mission,* February 1996, 2.

Chapter 10

1. The story was told by John Nielson, president of Asia-Pacific Nazarene Theological Seminary in Manila.

2. Chuck Colson, *The Body* (Dallas: Word, Inc., 1992), 385-409. All rights reserved.

Chapter 12

1. In this chapter, "world" will mean both the physical creation itself and the totality of the contexts and structures within which human life occurs. In the second sense, humanity and world are the two sides of one reality. If this be true, then redemption of humanity must include the world. Only a highly abstract definition of "human" could allow us to conclude otherwise.

2. Read Hal Lindsey's *The Late Great Planet Earth,* one of a host of expressions of current "Christian" doomsday pessimism.

3. Hendrikus Berkhof, *Christian Faith,* trans. Sierd Woudstra (Grand Rapids: Wm. B. Eerdmans, 1996), 512.

Chapter 13

1. In this chapter the word "finitude" will appear often. The word is simply the noun form of the adjective "finite." "Finitude" is one way of naming our creatureliness. Like all other things that exist, humans are bound by time and space. In spite of our rational powers, we are vulnerable and limited. Finitude means that we are dispensable—we don't have to exist.

2. Jurgen Moltmann, *The Experiment Hope* (Philadelphia: Fortress Press, 1975), 45.